The Old-House Doctor

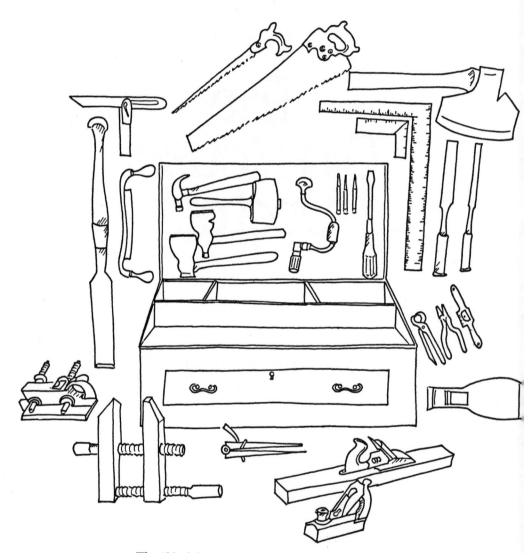

The "black bag" of an old time old-house doctor

The Old-House Doctor

The Essential Guide to Repairing, Restoring, and Rejuvenating Your Old Home

Christopher Evers

Illustrated by
HARRIET HASON

Skyhorse Publishing

Publisher's disclaimer:
This is a reprint of the 1986 edition of the book. The publisher and the author have agreed to leave the book in its original form, as the basic information herein has not changed. Please consult your local home improvement store or online for updated pricing and materials when necessary.

Skyhorse Publishing books may be purchased in bulk at special discounts for sales promotion, corporate gifts, fund-raising, or educational purposes. Special editions can also be created to specifications. For details, contact the Special Sales Department, Skyhorse Publishing, 307 West 36th Street, 11th Floor, New York, NY 10018 or info@skyhorsepublishing.com.

Skyhorse® and Skyhorse Publishing® are registered trademarks of Skyhorse Publishing, Inc.®, a Delaware corporation.

Visit our website at www.skyhorsepublishing.com.

10 9 8 7 6 5 4

Library of Congress Cataloging-in-Publication Data is available on file.

ISBN: 978-1-62087-369-4

Printed in the United States of America

To my children, Monir and Ivar

Contents

Acknowledgments

The path from original idea to completed book can be narrow and tortuous, with chasms of failure on either hand. This book would surely have perished in the abyss if it weren't for the following qualities of its collaborators and supporters; the incredible diligence and good humor of Harriet Hason, the patience and cooperation of the late Mr. Alfred Mayer, Peter, Merle, Mark, Irwin and everyone else at Overlook, the understanding and encouragement of my entire family, and especially the helpfulness of my father and my sister Jane, the early enthusiasm and support of Dakin Morehouse and Mel Ringstrom, the encouragement and constructive criticism of Mildred Reid, Bert English and all my other friends at Contoocook, the helpfulness of the Woodstock, Kingston Area, New York Public and New Hampshire State libraries.

The Old-House Doctor and His Patients

During my twenty-one years of professional old-house rehabilitation, I have often laid aside my tools for a moment to ponder the peculiar fascination that old-houses hold for so many people, including myself. Some people's relationships with them are easily expressed in dollars and cents, for older structures *do* offer strong financial enticements, such as low purchase price, powerful tax incentives, and the possibility of government grants. Others just find old-houses aesthetically more appealing than new ones. The love that many of us have for them is nevertheless not so easily explained, for it's rooted more deeply than the attraction inspired by money or beauty.

What then *could* be the cause of such a powerful feeling? This question has always plagued me, never yielding to an explanation without leaving new questions in its wake. My choice of professions has particularly perplexed me, ever since the day I gave up my college studies in order to learn the skills required to ease the sufferings of disease-stricken old-houses. This perplexity was greatly increased by the apparent disparity between my chosen profession and the predictions of a curious examination I took as a college freshman.

This prophecy was furnished by the Strong Vocational Interest Test, which asked interminable numbers of seemingly irrelevant questions such as, "Are you afraid of spiders?" and "Do you like people with gold teeth?" My answers to such questions demonstrated to my testers' satisfaction that the profession of doctor was my first vocational preference, while that of carpenter was my very last. It was

The peculiar fascination of an old-house

thus extremely puzzling to me when I shortly thereafter felt compelled to leave college and obstinately enroll myself in the study of old-house carpentry!

My testers' conclusions became increasingly mystifying to me as the years passed. I learned the trades of carpenter, painter, plumber, and electrician; yet I seemed no closer to being a doctor than when I'd left college. It wasn't until I began to share my old-house experience in the act of writing this book, that the enigma finally became clear to me. My testers had been inscrutably correct all along, for I now realized they had never promised there would be an M.D. after my name, but merely that I wished to be a *doctor*. And I had been one for many years without being aware of it—an *old-house doctor!*

My previously inexplicable feeling for old-houses was at last clear to me: I had for many years treated my old-house patients almost as if they had really been human beings. I'd diagnosed their illnesses, prescribed and administered appropriate courses of treatment for these and had taken great pleasure in watching them grow healthy again. I now look forward to sharing these satisfying years with you and hope they will help you to accord your old-house the care it so richly deserves.

Although the material in this book is largely limited to my personal experience, I have endeavored throughout to make it equally applicable to all old-houses, be they Eastern or Western, urban or rural, pre-Revolutionary or Victorian. It would nevertheless be as foolish for me to claim that I will tell you all you might want to know about your old-house as it would for an M.D. to assert that he had included the entire practice of medicine in one short volume. I do hope that I will answer many of your questions about your old-house and will direct you to many more in the extensive annotated bibliography at the end of the book. Yet I would consider my effort more than worthwhile if I succeeded in no more than imparting to you but a portion of the love and understanding of old-houses that my patients have inspired in me.

I had treated my old-house patients almost as if they had really been human beings.

CHAPTER

1

The Body and Soul
of the Old-House

Have you ever been powerfully attracted to an old-house without quite knowing why? You will open the door to an understanding of this mysterious attraction when you become aware of the unusual relationship between an old-house and the human body. As strange as it may seem, the two so closely parallel each other in so many details of their anatomies and physiologies that they often may be thought of as nearly interchangeable.

Perhaps this may come as less of a surprise when you consider that each of us carries a prototype or model for a certain dwelling deep within the darkest refuges of our memories. We all began life with a nine-month lease on this home, which was perhaps a trifle small and dimly lit; but these shortcomings were more than made up for by the benevolence of the landlady.

This lease was unfortunately nonrenewable and at its term we were summarily evicted by the formerly compassionate owner—leaving us unprotected and homeless. Since we couldn't survive for long in this condition, the old-house was gradually conceived by untold generations of human architects as a haven for our vulnerability. It thus came to surround us with a protective *skin*, usually supported by a wooden *skeleton* and inevitably pierced with holes through which light, sound, food, and air might enter. It had even acquired by the dawn of the 20th century, in the words of Frank Lloyd Wright, *"bowels, circulation, and nerves."*

If an old-house can be considered an outer body in which *our* bodies may live, what provision does it make for the sheltering of our spirits or souls? No such

1

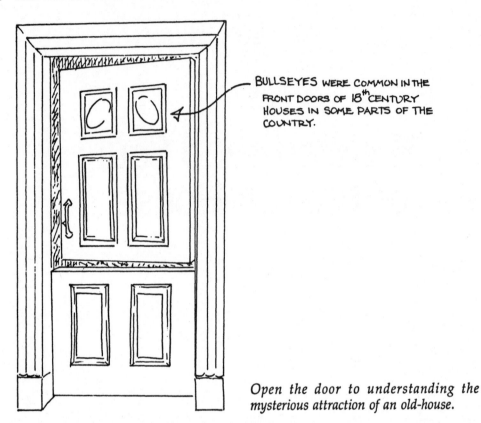

BULLSEYES WERE COMMON IN THE FRONT DOORS OF 18ᵗʰ CENTURY HOUSES IN SOME PARTS OF THE COUNTRY.

Open the door to understanding the mysterious attraction of an old-house.

shelter is provided by some otherwise excellent structures that somehow lack the intangible quality that allows us to feel truly at home in them. Most old-houses nonetheless welcome human spirits and give their inhabitants an extraordinary feeling of peace, wholeness, and belonging.

Perhaps the best way to understand this potent yet extremely elusive feeling and its cause is to take a trip through an old-house—from end to end, front to back, and bottom to top. Investigate every room, closet, and cupboard. Walk up and down every staircase. Open your senses to the house, but quiet your mind; take everything in, but don't evaluate or judge it at this time. Poke about up in the attic or in the top of the tower; look out of the windows and listen to the wind, traffic, or silence. What does it feel like up there? Now go all the way downstairs to the cellar; go into its furthest recesses and investigate murky shadows, cobwebs, and mold. Sit down in the dark for a while. What does it smell like there? Do you find it frightening or peaceful?

Did you feel different parts of yourself respond to the different levels of the old-house? We all live most of our waking hours in a busy state of mind, primarily concerned with the mechanics of our survival. This part of us should be at home on the living floors of a house. When we go to sleep and dream, however, another

What does it feel like in the attic?

level of our mind emerges—sometimes a very frightening one, yet at other times a deeply satisfying one. This part of us should be at its ease down in the cellar.

There are also moments in our lives when we feel above and beyond either our usual waking or dreaming state and when we are capable of seeing into the heart of things with astonishing clarity. This last part of us is at its best way up at the top of the house, in its attic or tower.

Did you feel excited, expectant, or afraid when you opened a certain door or went down a particular flight of stairs in the old-house? Doorways and staircases have a peculiarly significant effect on us, for they aren't only physical means to get from one part of a house to another. They are also the means of access to the various parts and levels of the soul of the old-house.

For this reason, the vast preponderance of legends, rituals, and superstitions pertaining to old-houses have to do with either doors or stairs. Ghosts appear to spend most of their time tramping up and down the staircases and opening and closing the doors of the houses they have chosen to haunt. The early American colonists therefore often made it their practice to inscribe their door latches with hex marks to keep evil spirits from passing through.

They also sometimes constructed secret doorways, staircases, and small rooms, the purpose of which was ostensibly to help them flee or hide from Indians or the British (or to hide runaway slaves); yet long after these purposes have vanished, their mysterious charm survives. Imagine your feelings if you unwittingly tripped a hidden latch and found yourself on the brink of a narrow, dark, and winding flight of stairs or a room secret to all but its population of rodents, insects, and spiders!

An old-house doesn't necessarily have to date back to colonial times for it to have its share of secrets; I recently uncovered a hidden staircase in a house constructed in the 1880s. It hadn't begun its life as secret, but had merely been considered superfluous by one of its owners, who had consequently boarded it up. With the excitement of an archaeologist entering a newly discovered tomb, I tore up a suspicious patch in the dining room floor of this house and descended the cobweb-choked staircase thus revealed. My progress was soon stopped at the foot of the steps by a blank wall; but this soon yielded to hammer and bar, and I found myself in the old cellar kitchen.

Sit down in the cellar for a while . . .

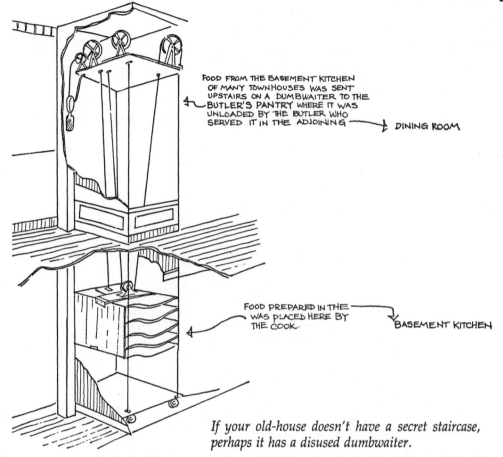

FOOD FROM THE BASEMENT KITCHEN
OF MANY TOWNHOUSES WAS SENT
UPSTAIRS ON A DUMBWAITER TO THE
BUTLER'S PANTRY WHERE IT WAS
UNLOADED BY THE BUTLER WHO
SERVED IT IN THE ADJOINING ——— DINING ROOM

FOOD PREPARED IN THE
WAS PLACED HERE BY
THE COOK.

BASEMENT KITCHEN

If your old-house doesn't have a secret staircase, perhaps it has a disused dumbwaiter.

Such hidden parts of old-house anatomy await their rediscovery by those of us who care to seek them out. Always be on the lookout for any unusual thicknesses in the walls of an old-house, particularly in partitions and around chimneys. These may yield no greater secret than an abandoned airshaft, dumbwaiter, or pipe chase (a space in a wall specifically designed for plumbing or wiring), yet it's always possible that one of the building's most intimate secrets may be disclosed to you.

Once you've become truly familiar with your old-house, its anatomical, physiological, and spiritual relationship to the human body and soul should become apparent. The correspondence doesn't end here, however, for old-houses deteriorate with age and poor maintenance in exactly the same manner as do our bodies. They are likewise subject to many of the same types of injuries and diseases to which we ourselves are prone, be they dislocations, fractures, infections, or infestations of parasites.

The diagnostic and therapeutic techniques that may be used to treat the complaints of an old-house are furthermore often quite similar to those utilized by doctors to cure our own ailments. The number of old-houses actually receiving such expert medical attention is, nevertheless, unfortunately very small; for the profession of old-house doctor isn't nearly so glamorous or lucrative as that of the medical doctor and consequently doesn't normally attract the most skilled or dedicated practitioners.

There is little doubt that working on old-houses is far dirtier, less predictable, and less efficient than on new ones. It's therefore not surprising that many

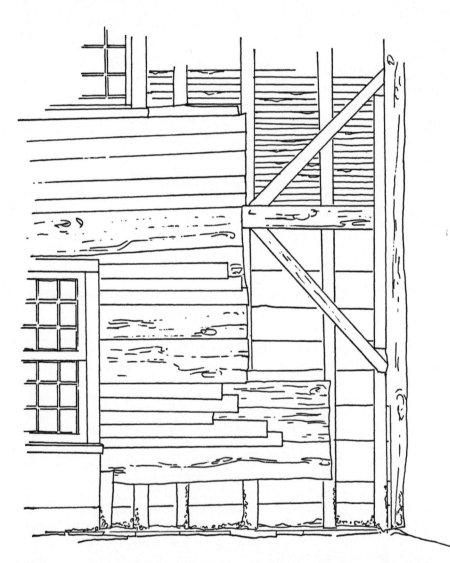

Old-house work may be dirty and unpredictable, but its rewards more than make up for it.

tradespeople think of an old-house solely in terms of the number of obstacles it will throw in their paths to quick efficient work and good profit. One country contractor of my acquaintance went so far as to instruct me that "There are only *two* ways to work on an old-house—one's with a bulldozer and the other's with a match."

Traditionally many architects have been almost as unenthusiastic about old-house commissions unless they involve buildings of great antiquity or exceptional historic interest. Their frequent insensitivity to old-houses under their care is nevertheless not wholly inexplicable: What serious artist would be eager to rework a canvas another painter had begun? Many architects have simply succumbed to the temptation to "paint" the old work out and begin again with their own design.

There has nevertheless been a most encouraging trend in recent years toward greater appreciation of old-houses on the part of all who come in contact with them. This has largely been brought about by the astronomical increase in the cost of new construction, necessitating a far more sympathetic reevaluation of diseased and dying structures. There are consequently many carpenters, plumbers, and architects who now welcome old-house work, wisely realizing that in an uncertain building market an old-house is certainly better than no house at all!

This climate of old-house appreciation is thus perfectly genuine but somewhat limited in scope. If you want your old-house to get the very best medical attention, *you* are going to have to learn to be its doctor. This doesn't mean you actually have to do all the work yourself, for it's perfectly possible for you to obtain the competent and even inspired services of carpenter, plumber, and architect. But don't expect your carpenter to appreciate the singing of the wind in your tower or your architect to know or care what it smells like in your cellar. These specialists have enough to do to perform their own tasks quickly and competently. It's up to you to supply the overview that will hasten the recovery and safeguard the health of the body and soul of your old-house.

2

Exposing the Secrets of Your Old-House's Past

On your first visit, a doctor will usuallyhave you fill out a form that will supply such information as your name, age, and medical history. This data gives a background against which to view the results of the subsequent physical examination. An old-house doctor requires much the same sort of information, but as the old-house is unable to fill out a form for you, you must gather it yourself.

Who built your house? When did they build it and for whom? What is the architectural style of your house? Who lived in it and what were their lives like? When and how were the various additions, alterations, and repairs made to your house? The answers to these and many more such questions may prove invaluable in assisting you to correctly prescribe a course of treatment for your old-house.

How much time you're willing to spend uncovering the secrets of your house's past is of course up to you, but it should be determined in some measure by its age, value, and personality. Probing the past can be very time consuming, but may also be quite fascinating and at times unexpectedly rewarding. A friend of mine once bought an old farmhouse in Maine, in the cellar of which he unearthed several dozen very rare old bottles, which he actually sold for more than he had paid for the house! Everyone can't expect to be as lucky as he, but it would be unlucky indeed if you find or learn nothing of value in your exploration of your

8 old-house's past.

What Maps, Papers, and Photographs Can Tell You

Your old-house probably has some good friends among the old people of your community, who could tell you much of value once you get them talking about it. Old people usually love to talk about the past, but sometimes it's difficult to get them started. It helps not to appear *too* eager to get specific information from them—let them tell their own stories in their own way and time. You may hear much irrelevant information this way, but some of this will in all likelihood be very interesting in its own right.

Old people's testimony may be the most important evidence you'll find, but it also may be completely misleading due to lapses of memory or distortions of fact. You might think you'd found the perfect informant in an old man with long white beard who had lived on the hill behind your house for the past eighty-nine years. "To be sure, that's the old Keegan house," he might tell you, "built long before the Revolution!" Upon subsequent investigation, it may turn out that a person named Coogan once owned the structure in the 1860s and that it was actually built in

Documentary evidence needn't be dry and dull: look for the story between the lines!

1822. As old as your informant was, he was still merely speculating about what had occurred long before he was around to witness it.

Such oral testimony should therefore always be verified by documentary evidence. Written records pertaining to your old-house may be located in a variety of places, depending on what part of the country you live in and whether you are an urban or rural dweller. It is for this reason very advantageous for you to find someone who is familiar with the local sources of such material, such as your local librarian, member of the buildings department or landmark preservation commission, town or county historian, president of your local historical society, or your town or county clerk.

In case you're unable to locate such a person who is willing to give you the assistance you need, I've compiled the following listing of possible sources of documentary information pertaining to your old-house:

Deeds: The county courthouse is the repository of all deeds in most parts of the country, but several states (such as Connecticut and Vermont) keep them at the town clerk's office. All deeds are indexed both by the grantor (seller) and the grantee (buyer) of a property. They sometimes contain useful descriptions of buildings located on the lot or acreage conveyed. Each deed will usually refer to a prior conveyance, making it possible to trace the transfer of title to your property back through the years to its very first owner (provided all deeds were recorded, or officially submitted to the clerk's office and weren't subsequently lost or destroyed).

Probate Records: These are also generally filed at the county courthouse and include such documents as wills, administrator's accounts, and inventories. An inventory of the deceased's possessions was commonly made if he or she died intestate (left no will) which may prove very interesting to you.

Tax Records: Such records may be found in the offices of the town or county clerk or at city hall.

Town Registers: Some towns published annual listings of the names and addresses of all their residents.

Census Records: The federal government began taking the census at ten-year intervals in 1790. Later censuses include the name of every member of the household, the occupation of the head of it, and the value of the real estate. Some of these are available at the local county clerk's office, but almost all are on microfilm in the National Archives in Washington, D.C.

Court Records: Sometimes disputes involving real estate caused detailed information concerning buildings and land to be recorded in the files of various courts. These records are scattered about—ask a local lawyer for their locations.

Insurance Policies: A fire insurance policy taken out on your old-house many years ago might be a valuable find, for it would represent the house's equivalent of a life insurance policy and would consequently contain information on its health and age.

County Histories: Many county histories were published during the last quarter of the 19th century that included biographical sketches of "prominent citizens" and lithographs of their homes. The accuracy of the sketches was unfortunately not always very great, which isn't to be wondered at when one realizes that the "prominent citizens" paid the publisher to be included in the volume. The lithographs of their houses are nevertheless usually fairly accurate.

Family Genealogies: If you're lucky enough to have a house that was owned by a family with a published family tree, it should shed some light on the succession of ownership of the structure. A useful bibliography of published genealogies is *Genealogies in the Library of Congress.*

County Atlases and Wall Maps: County atlases often listed the name of every house-owner in the county but are subject to the same limitations as county histories. Wall maps often have insets with pictures of prominent houses. To locate these atlases and maps, try your local library or historical society.

Surveyors' Maps: These often contain more information about very early houses than deeds. They usually indicate the specific location of an old-house on its land and sometimes include intriguing details, such as the building's number of chimneys. Surveyors' maps may be found in manuscript depositories at county clerks' offices, in the offices of surveyors and lawyers, and in the libraries of local historical societies.

Architect's Drawings: If your old-house was designed by an architect, it's quite possible the original plans and elevations are on file at the architectural firm's offices (if they still are in business).

Town or City Histories and Historical Society Publications: Check your library for these, for they might contain information on your old-house or may lead you to other sources of use to you.

Account Books, Journals, Purchase Orders, etc.: The records kept by general stores or hardware, lumber, and household furnishing dealers may contain invaluable data on the materials used to build or repair your old-house and the items supplied to furnish it. Check the local historical society for them.

Old Newspapers: They may contain reports of important events in the life of your old-house, such as its birth or injury by fire. They may be found (usually on microfilm) at your local library, the state library, the state historical society's library, or the local newspaper's own office. If you're unable to locate the early issues of a newspaper, consult the *Union List of Newspapers* at your library.

Letters and Diaries: They could contain priceless material relevant to your old-house. Look for them in libraries and historical societies and ask long-time residents of your community if they might have any in their possession.

Postcards, Photographs, and Stereoscopic (three-dimensional) Views: Photographs and stereoscopic views came on the scene around the middle of the 19th century, while postcards lagged about twenty years behind. Stereoscopic views passed out of vogue around the turn of the century, however, while photographs and postcards are obviously still popular today. All of these could provide you with a picture of your old-house during the late 19th or early 20th century.

Finding Buried Treasures: Old-House Archaeology

Archaeology isn't usually considered to be a subject of interest to the old-house owner, but its importance shouldn't be overlooked. There are three excellent reasons why you should consider digging: (1) It's an exciting and enjoyable pastime; (2) You *might* unearth a pot of gold coins, a heap of rare old bottles, or other valuable artifacts; and (3) You're sure to learn many fascinating details about the history and personality of your old-house—information obtainable in no other way.

Of course nothing could just be exciting, enjoyable, potentially profitable, and educational with no strings attached, and archaeology is certainly no exception. A badly managed "dig" is far worse than none at all, because it destroys evidence an archaeologist might have been able to gather at some future time. If

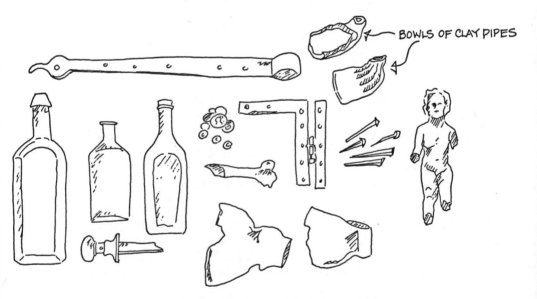

Some of the artifacts unearthed at one old-house

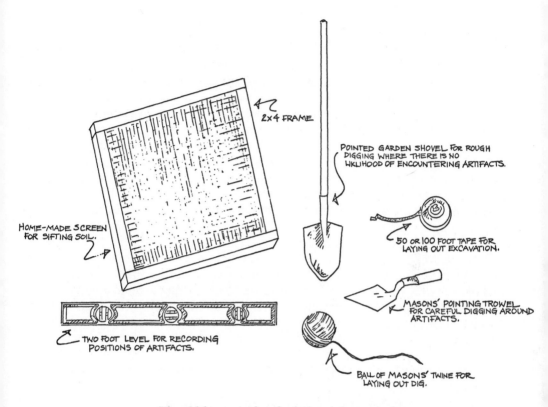

2×4 FRAME

POINTED GARDEN SHOVEL FOR ROUGH
DIGGING WHERE THERE IS NO
LIKLIHOOD OF ENCOUNTERING ARTIFACTS.

HOME-MADE SCREEN
FOR SIFTING SOIL.

50 OR 100 FOOT TAPE FOR
LAYING OUT EXCAVATION.

MASONS' POINTING TROWEL
FOR CAREFUL DIGGING AROUND
ARTIFACTS.

TWO FOOT LEVEL FOR RECORDING
POSITIONS OF ARTIFACTS.

BALL OF MASONS' TWINE FOR
LAYING OUT DIG.

The old-house archaeologist's minimum tools

you're to have a good conscience, you must therefore exercise extreme caution in this matter: There are times when only a qualified team of professionals should undertake the job.

Most old-house sites would nevertheless never be excavated by professional archaeologists and thus are fair game for the amateur. This is particularly true when the ground is going to be disturbed anyway, as when an addition is about to be built or a drainfield replaced. Digging in such a case would be salvage archaeology and even the most mistrustful of professionals would have to concede that an amateur with a shovel could do no more damage to a site than a backhoe or bulldozer.

I must have nonetheless come remarkably close to rivaling the destructive energy of these machines in the misguided enthusiasm of my first archaeological effort. I was so excited by finding my first artifact (a most interesting old bottle) that I went into a frenzy of digging—haphazardly throwing shovelsful of dirt in all directions. After several hours of this exhilaration, I realized I was hopelessly "lost," for I didn't know where I had excavated and where I hadn't. I furthermore had no notion of the location and depth at which any artifact had been found and many of them had been broken or lost in my excitement.

This kind of activity is the very antithesis of archaeology—the professionals call it artifact- or pot-hunting and consider it to be nothing short of sacrilegious. They have excellent justification for feeling this way, as countless prime archaeological sites worldwide have been ruthlessly looted by seekers of fortunes or collectibles. The archaeologists' complaint isn't the loss to them of these treasures, but rather that they were removed in a totally unscientific manner.

The fundamental precept of archaeology is to excavate so systematically that the process could actually be reversed, each artifact being returned to its original location and covered with the same soil—just like a movie run backward. It's obvious that to achieve such a result would necessitate the most meticulous written and photographic records of the precise positions of all artifacts before they are removed from the excavation. With such records at their disposal, archaeologists are able to reconstruct the events that long ago left their telltale signs, which were covered by the earthy accumulations of ensuing years.

Thus both pot-hunters and archaeologists unearth artifacts, but only the latter uncover the past. As an old-house owner, you shouldn't be content with merely retrieving objects from the ground, but should be curious to learn the whole story they have to tell. Let's suppose you are going to build an addition to your old-house and find a wrought iron hinge and fragments of very old pottery under a lilac bush you are transplanting from the site. If you have the curiosity of an archaeologist, you will immediately want to know all that piece of ground can tell you. Was the area long ago used as a dump or an Indian camp? Could it have been the site of a building older than your house? Was a Revolutionary War battle held upon it?

In order to give you an idea of whether the area is archaeologically worth excavating, you may first dig several other small test pits, probe the ground with a long iron rod, or go over the area with a metal detector. If the results of one or more of these tests seem promising, you'd better start digging right away, before the backhoe comes to excavate the cellar hole for your addition in its own insensitive manner.

If you are a true archaeologist at heart, you will delineate the area before you dig with stakes and mason's twine in the form of a rectangle (easily checked by making certain that it has equal opposite sides and diagonals). The location of each artifact you uncover may now be recorded in a notebook, including its position relative to the sides of the rectangle and its depth (of far greater importance than its horizontal position) beneath the surface of the ground. All that remains to be done is to record the distance and direction of one of the rectangle's corners from a fixed location known as a datum point, such as the corner of your house. You may now proceed to dig up your buried treasures without fear that the archaeologist who may be lurking behind your hedge will suddenly hurl the terrible epithet "pot-hunter!" at you.

By the time you finish excavating your archaeological site, you will hopefully have myriads of neatly bagged and labeled artifacts of all descriptions. Now it is time to try to piece together the fascinating story that they may tell. Suppose that

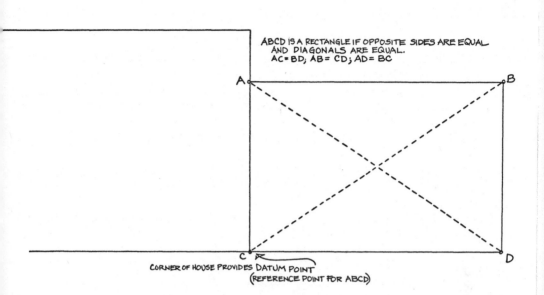

ABCD IS A RECTANGLE IF OPPOSITE SIDES ARE EQUAL AND DIAGONALS ARE EQUAL.
AC = BD; AB = CD; AD = BC

CORNER OF HOUSE PROVIDES DATUM POINT (REFERENCE POINT FOR ABCD)

How to lay out a rectangle for an archaeological dig (or an addition)

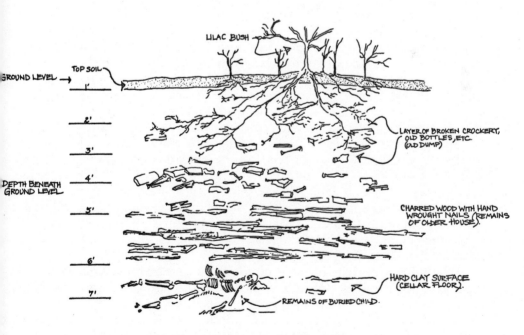

LILAC BUSH

GROUND LEVEL → TOP SOIL
1'
2'
3'
DEPTH BENEATH GROUND LEVEL
4'
5'
6'
7'

LAYER OF BROKEN CROCKERY, OLD BOTTLES, ETC. (OLD DUMP)

CHARRED WOOD WITH HAND WROUGHT NAILS (REMAINS OF OLDER HOUSE).

HARD CLAY SURFACE (CELLAR FLOOR).

REMAINS OF BURIED CHILD.

The story beneath the lilac bush

from about 1' to 5' below the surface, you encountered a layer of broken crockery, old bottles, and animal bones mixed with assorted debris and detritus. Directly beneath this layer, you uncovered a foot-thick mantle of charred wood, containing many hand-wrought nails. After this a hard-packed clay surface, at which point you nearly abandoned your downward momentum, but persisting 2' more you uncovered an entire human skeleton of diminutive size!

The story such a collection of artifacts and *their relationship to each other* might tell could be as follows: A house much older than your own may once have occupied your site, but it long ago burned to the ground and its cellar hole was for many years used as a dump. The hard-packed clay surface you encountered was the cellar floor of this house and the skeleton was that of a child buried long ago beneath that floor during a particularly ferocious winter or so as to provide the house with a benevolent spirit!

Your Old-House's Class or Architectural Style

Although the history of American architectural styles is a fascinating subject in its own right, its importance to the owners of most old-houses has been grossly exaggerated. If you *can* determine your house's architectural status you will have an excellent indication of its age, but you must resist the temptation to think of its style in the same terms we might think of a person's class, religion, or color. In both cases we downgrade the uniqueness of the individual in the process of concentrating on their groups.

Determining your old-house's architectural style is moreover often not that easy a task, for the majority of old-houses stubbornly resist such classification. Very few of them were designed and built in their entirety at one particular time or with any unified architectural concept. Most old-houses just grew over the years in response to the needs of their owners and the capabilities of their builders, often becoming in the process highly individualistic architectural composites.

This important fact was quaintly expressed by one A. Rowden King in his handbook for real estate salespersons. In a chapter of this work entitled "How to sell hybrids and houses you cannot identify," Mr. King asserts that "There are far more houses that simply cannot be classified architecturally than those that can be. A rough estimate might be that 75% of all houses are unclassifiable, just as most dogs are unclassifiable." If Mr. King is right, three out of four old-houses would thus be unclassifiable mongrels with no greater social status than their canine counterparts.

Why is this fact so hard for many of us to accept? Americans have always been extremely sensitive about their antecedents, be they genealogical or architectural. Most of us are after all descended from immigrants who were either paupers, refugees, slaves, heretics, or criminals. Our architectural heritage doesn't appear to be any more impressive to the purist, who therefore has grossly exaggerated the importance of American style in order to confer respectability on it.

COLONIAL 1690-1760

GEORGIAN 1720-1780

FEDERAL 1780-1820

GOTHIC REVIVAL 1835-1880

GREEK REVIVAL 1815-1840

QUEEN ANNE 1875-1900

MANSARD 1855-1885

ITALIANATE 1845-1885

TWENTIETH CENTURY "MODERN c 1930

Some of the most distinctive architectural styles

The settlers of the New England and Chesapeake Bay colonies brought their architectural traditions with them from England, the Pennsylvania Dutch brought theirs from Germany and the colonists of New York state from Holland and France. These traditions remained strong for about two hundred years, changing only slightly to accommodate themselves to the new environment. Then during the 19th century a great explosion of interest in other architectural styles took place. This was largely due to the fact that the United States had by then become an autonomous and increasingly powerful young nation with ever-expanding channels of communication with the rest of the world and ever-enlarging sources of raw materials and skilled labor.

Americans seemed determined to develop their own architectural style during that century but went about it in such a manner as to excite widespread accusations of plagiarism. American architects brazenly "borrowed" architectural themes and embellishments from around the world and through the ages. This

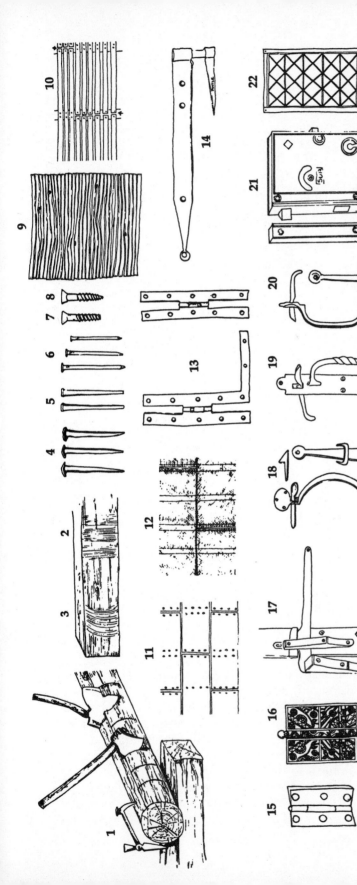

Appendix 2: Keys to the dating of old houses

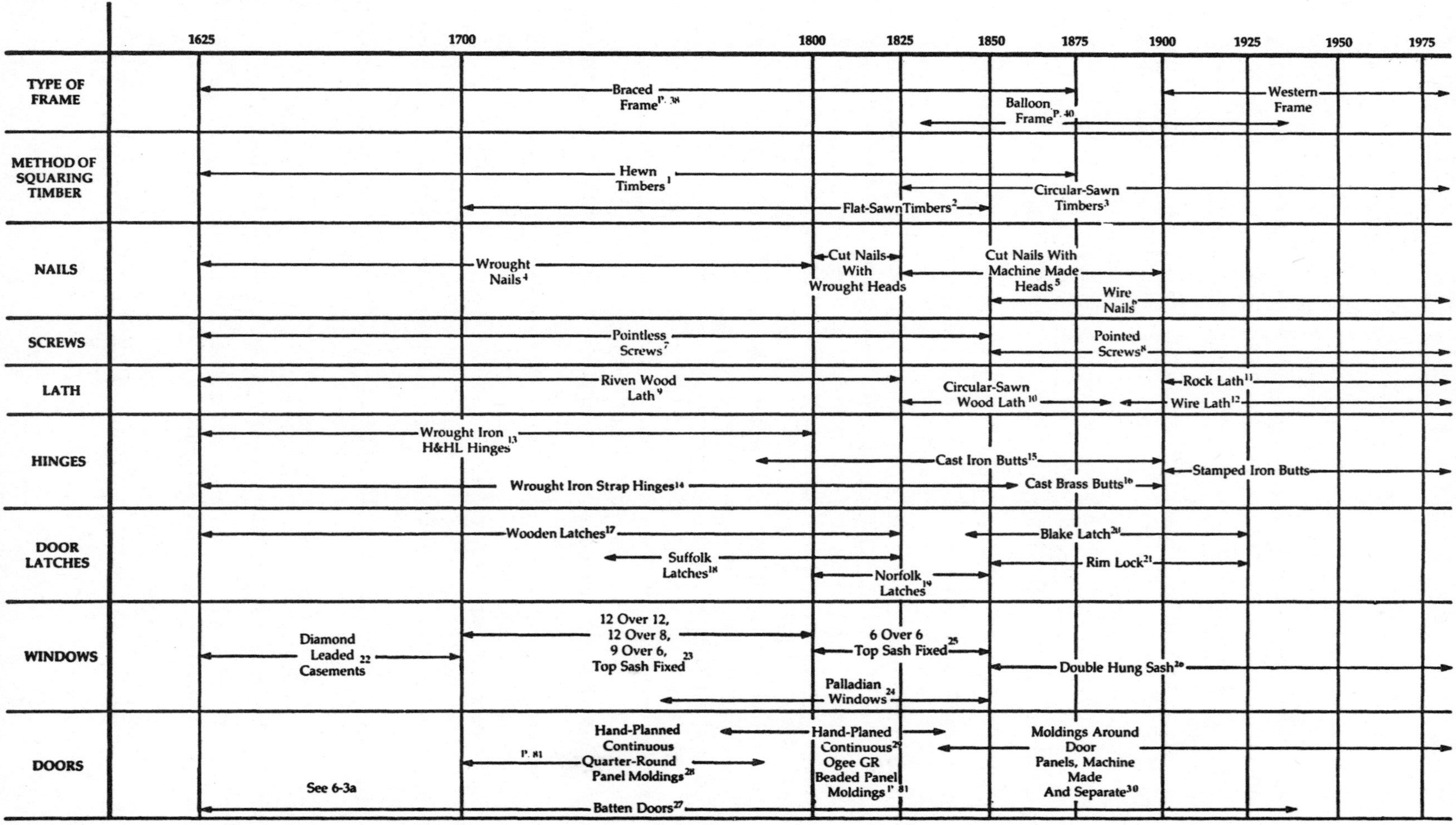

Timeline scale (top): 1625 — 1700 — 1800 — 1825 — 1850 — 1875 — 1900 — 1925 — 1950 — 1975

TYPE OF FRAME
- Braced Frame p.38
- Balloon Frame p.40
- Western Frame

METHOD OF SQUARING TIMBER
- Hewn Timbers
- Flat-Sawn Timbers²
- Circular-Sawn Timbers³

NAILS
- Wrought Nails⁴
- Cut Nails With Wrought Heads
- Cut Nails With Machine Made Heads⁵
- Wire Nails⁶

SCREWS
- Pointless Screws⁷
- Pointed Screws⁸

LATH
- Riven Wood Lath⁹
- Circular-Sawn Wood Lath¹⁰
- Rock Lath¹¹
- Wire Lath¹²

HINGES
- Wrought Iron H&HL Hinges¹³
- Wrought Iron Strap Hinges¹⁴
- Cast Iron Butts¹⁵
- Cast Brass Butts¹⁶
- Stamped Iron Butts

DOOR LATCHES
- Wooden Latches¹⁷
- Suffolk Latches¹⁸
- Norfolk Latches¹⁹
- Blake Latch²⁰
- Rim Lock²¹

WINDOWS
- Diamond Leaded Casements²²
- 12 Over 12, 12 Over 8, 9 Over 6, Top Sash Fixed²³
- Palladian Windows²⁴
- 6 Over 6 Top Sash Fixed²⁵
- Double Hung Sash²⁶

DOORS
- See 6-3a
- Batten Doors²⁷
- Hand-Planned Continuous Quarter-Round Panel Moldings²⁸ p.81
- Hand-Planed Continuous Ogee GR Beaded Panel Moldings¹ ³¹
- Moldings Around Door Panels, Machine Made And Separate³⁰

eclecticism was long thought of as a senseless cacophony of conflicting and superfluous confusion, but is at last being appreciated for what it is—a bold and original architectural symphony. What after all could an American style of architecture be but a composite of the incredibly varied heritages of the American people?

If you have an old-house that really appears to represent a pure architectural style or (which is far more likely) parts of it do and you are curious as to this style(s), I don't mean to thwart your curiosity. The accompanying illustration depicts nine of the commonest American architectural styles and their times of vogue. If you wish to go into the subject in greater depth, I've listed several excellent works in the Bibliography that will certainly enable you to do so.

How to Persuade Your Old-House to Divulge its Age

If you were unusually fortunate, you have already determined the exact birthdate of your old-house during your quest for oral and documentary evidence. It's nevertheless more likely that you obtained far less specific information. You might typically have discovered that your old-house was definitely alive in 1896, a building existed on the same site in 1847 and that the lot was vacant in 1801. Perhaps your archaeological exploration and your determination of your old-house's architectural style have supplied further clues, but you're still far from being able to assign it a definite birthdate.

It's time now to turn to your old-house itself to see if you can persuade it to divulge its age to you. This is seldom so simple as finding an inscription on a beam, stating that "John Carpenter Built This Fine House In The Year Of Our Lord Seventeen Hundred And Three." You might be so lucky, but you will more likely have to assess carefully a great many details of construction, often insignificant in themselves, yet of great consequence when considered collectively. In order to help you in this endeavor, I've compiled a table of indicative architectural details and their time-spans of popularity (See Table 5).

You must take care when using this table not to attribute undue importance to one or two uncorroborated indicators. Suppose you discover a door in your old-house hung with H-L hinges: Would you be correct in assuming your house was built prior to 1800? Even though this particular piece of evidence appears to validate this assumption, it's not justified for the following reasons:

1. The door and its hardware might have been salvaged from a much earlier house and recycled for economic or aesthetic considerations.

2. The hinges might be handmade reproductions of the originals, perhaps of considerable age themselves.

3. They may have been forged long after their period of common usage by an elderly back-country blacksmith who hadn't yet accepted the new styles.

Nor is it correct to assume that an old-house furnished with Blake patent thumb latches couldn't have been built before 1840 when the latches were patented. It would have been all too easy for someone to change the door hardware in an 18th-century house during the course of an extensive 19th-century remodeling.

You should thus never jump to conclusions on the basis of one or two indicators, but if a number of them substantiate each other, you may feel more confident in drawing specific inferences from them. This is particularly true when their evidence corroborates your earlier documentary research and/or archaeological digging. You should also give greater weight to indicators from those portions of your house most likely to have resisted change over the years. These

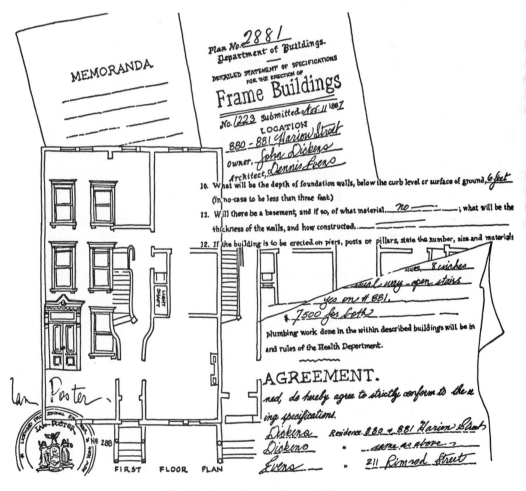

The birth certificate of one old-house

are invariably the places least likely to receive public scrutiny, such as the cellar and attic, while a room designed to receive and possibly impress company (such as the parlor) was often remodeled many times in order to keep up with changing fashions.

You can determine the dimensions of the sills and joists* of your house when you're in its cellar and whether they were hewn or sawn. You will also be able to view the underside of the first-floor floorboards (or sub-flooring), enabling you to note their width and whether they were planed, flat sawn, or circular sawn. If there are any doors or windows in your cellar, they (and their hinges and latches) are more likely to be original than any others in your house.

You can usually see the rafters in your attic and perhaps the plates* as well. If the rafters are hewn and are joined at the peak with a mortise-and-tenon* joint, your house was more than likely built prior to 1840. If they are circular sawn and meet a ridgeboard at the peak, it's unlikely that it was built before 1900. You can often tell how many times your house has been reroofed by a close examination of the shingle nails protruding through the undersides of the roofboards. Multiply this number by 30 (a conservative estimate of the longevity of a good cedar shingle roof) and you will have a fair indication of the age of your old-house.

From your observation of the many details of the construction of your old-house and your prior investigation of its past, you have by this time undoubtedly formed a pretty good opinion of its age. This won't even now be in all likelihood an *exact* date if your house is a very early one, but this needn't discourage you. The knowledge that an individual is an octogenarian or a teenager is usually sufficient to get a pretty clear picture of them—it doesn't matter too much if they're fourteen or fifteen, eighty-seven or eighty-eight. The younger your house, the more likely it is that you'll be able to determine its age with accuracy: if it's *only* about a hundred years old, you may even be so fortunate as to uncover its birth certificate.

*See page 39 for an explanation of these terms.

3

How Disease May Threaten Your Old-House

Now that you've examined your old-house from the perspectives of historian, archaeologist, and architect, it's time to assume the dispassionate demeanor of the old-house doctor and conduct a physical examination of the patient. You must ignore the beauty and appeal of your old-house for the present, for no matter what historical, architectural, or aesthetic merit it may possess, its physical condition is obviously of overriding importance. It matters little when your house was built or how elegant its design if it suffers from a terminal illness.

Old-house disease often conceals itself most deceptively (as do the maladies of used cars and human beings), often thriving where visibility and access are poorest. Even if a symptom is clearly visible, you're probably seeing but a small fraction of it—the vast bulk of the malady may lurk invisible and undetected. You must therefore prepare yourself to travel over, under, through, and around your house; you must investigate every seldom-seen nook and cranny, no matter how diminutive, dark, or dirty. Even the most thorough of such investigations would do you little good if you didn't know what to look for, however, so it's essential that you previously understand the nature of old-house disease.

Old-House Infections: The Ravages of Wet-Rot and the Myth of Dry-Rot

By far the most prevalent form of old-house disease is the decay of its wooden components. It may seem natural to you that wood should eventually rot—just as **23**

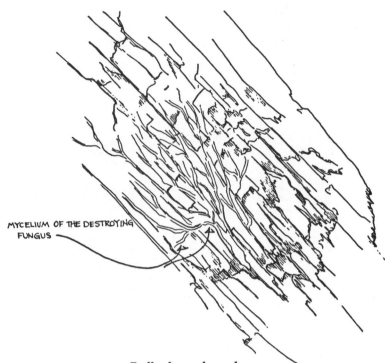

MYCELIUM OF THE DESTROYING FUNGUS

Badly decayed wood

iron rusts and rubber deteriorates with age—but the processes are entirely different. The deteriorations of these materials are the results of chemical reactions with the atmosphere, while the decay of wood is a *disease* caused by parasitic plants known as wood-destroying fungi. When wood is protected from these fungi, it won't significantly deteriorate in over a thousand years!

Fungi reproduce by generating microscopic "seeds" called spores that are light enough to be carried around the world by favorable air currents. The spore-producing capability of a fungus is incredible: a square yard of one of the common wood-destroyers produces up to nine hundred million of them every hour! Once a single spore has chanced upon a suitable host (such as a wooden beam in your old-house), it will germinate and sprout a tendril, which rapidly grows into a fabric called the fungi's mycelium. When this has grown to a sufficient mass within the body of its host, fruiting bodies will appear on the surface of the beam, in the form of mushrooms, crusts, brackets, or soft, pulpy masses. These are the reproductive organs of the fungus, whose function is to grow and discharge new spores, beginning its life cycle anew.

In order to complete this successfully, the fungus must not only find a suitable host but must also have a small amount of free oxygen, temperatures within certain limits, a suitable amount of moisture in, on, or around its host, and an absence of toxic substances. As every piece of wood in your house is a potential host for these fungi—and as oxygen is readily available to them—these factors are of no practical consequence to you in controlling their growth. It's nevertheless interesting to note that wood completely submerged in water or buried in the ground at depths of five or more feet will *never* decay, as the oxygen available to potentially destructive fungi is insufficient.

The optimum temperature for fungal growth is between 80°and 90° Fahrenheit. At temperatures higher or lower than this range, it slows down until it ceases altogether at the opposite extremes of 32° and 100° F. These temperature extremes don't kill the fungi but merely inhibit their growth. They live on in a state of suspended animation for years, waiting for a favorable break in the weather to resume their consumption of wood.

Fungi cannot consume wood having a moisture content of less than 20 percent and don't really have much of an appetite for it until it contains one-third of its capacity to hold water. Decay progresses more and more rapidly as the moisture content rises even higher, until the point at which the wood becomes completely saturated, when all decay abruptly ceases.

The reasons for this behavior become clear when we understand the manner in which fungi destroy wood. Most of them only consume the wood's cellulose (the principal constituent of wood) by injecting a digestive enzyme called cellulase into their host's sap ducts. Fungi are dependent on the moisture in these ducts to

This neglected old-house suffers from many diseases.

dissolve and disseminate this enzyme. The greater the moisture, the more rapidly they are able to penetrate and consume the wood—until it becomes totally saturated, at which point they perish for want of oxygen.

The ever-saturated sapwood of a living tree is protected against fungi in exactly this manner, but what of its sapless heartwood? The tree ingeniously protects this against decay by filling its empty sap ducts with natural preservatives and minerals that are toxic to fungi. Humans have utilized such heartwood for their constructions for thousands of years, particularly from trees that have developed unusually effective toxins. Cedar, locust, redwood, cypress, longleaf yellow pine, and the virtually extinct American chestnut all have singularly fungi-resistant heartwoods, but none of these (with rare local exceptions) are easy or cheap to acquire at this time.

It is therefore perhaps fortunate that we haven't contented ourselves with nature's gift and have formulated potent toxins of our own that may be used to render even the most vulnerable sapwood impervious to decay. Although the brush application of such wood preservatives as pentachlorophenol, Cuprinol, or creosote will definitely deter fungi, it's far from a foolproof measure. No matter how liberally you may apply them, they will never penetrate very deeply into the wood, leaving its center vulnerable to decay if but one spore finds its way through the toxic armor. Pressure-treated lumber, in which preservative has been forced under pressure to penetrate wood to its core, will provide no such access and will be virtually immune to the attack of wood-destroying fungi.

The problem with wood preservatives is that they are not only toxic to fungi but unfortunately to ourselves as well. The degree of hazard they pose the homeowner is as yet far from clear, but the toxic potentialities of such a chemical as pentachlorophenol (the active ingredient in many common preservatives) aren't to be taken lightly. Perhaps the most spine-chilling habit of chlorophenols is that of releasing dioxins (toxins 170,000 times more deadly than cyanide) when they are burned. Of course you wouldn't be planning to burn your wood preservative, but what would happen if your well-preserved house caught on fire?

Fortunately you may discourage wood-destroying fungi with no risk to yourself by exploiting their total dependence on a suitable supply of moisture to transmit their digestive enzymes. It's usually quite feasible to keep the moisture content in the wooden parts of an old-house at less than the 20 to 30 percent required by fungi to consume them. You should therefore never introduce wet or green wood into any area of your house in which fungi might thrive. You must likewise take every precaution to prevent wood already present in your house from becoming wet through contact with the earth, leaks in the roof or plumbing system, or by being confined in an unventilated area where condensation is likely to occur.

If you already have infestations of fungi, it's of paramount importance to remove their source of moisture as soon as possible. This is quite evident when the decaying wood is water-soaked and in contact with the ground or directly under a hole in the roof. But what if it looks dry and crumbly and isn't anywhere near an

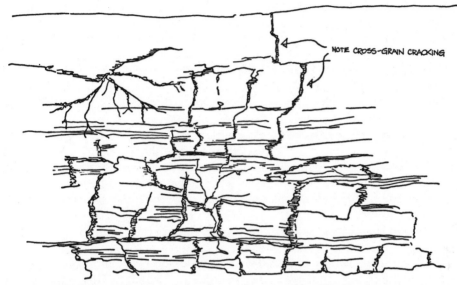

NOTE CROSS-GRAIN CRACKING

Wood afflicted with wet rot often has a dry, crumbly, checkered appearance.

apparent moisture source? Isn't this one of those terrible cases of the dreaded dry-rot you've heard about? Let me lay your mind at ease. *All* wood decay is caused by wood-destroying fungi, and *all* of these have exactly the same moisture requirements. There is no such thing as dry-rot.

The widespread belief in this mythical creature has come about through the failure of many of us to detect a fungus infestation's ultimate source of moisture. In most cases (such as those in ships' bilges and unventilated crawl spaces) this is simply the water vapor in the air, which under certain conditions (which may not exist when you inspect the area) condenses on the wood being decayed.

An even less obvious moisture source is utilized by two species of fungi that are actually capable of pumping their own water supply from up to thirty feet away from the wood they consume. One of these is a formidable threat to old-houses in the British Isles but only occasionally makes its appearance in the northernmost reaches of this country, due to its extreme sensitivity to summer heat. The other species is common on the Gulf Coast and in the Pacific Northwest, where it does extensive damage. If your house is in one of these areas and has a baffling fungus infestation without an apparent source of moisture, look for a ropelike pipe of mycelium leading from the afflicted wood to the ground or a leaky drain.

Old-House Parasites: The Terrible Termite and Its Associates

Wood-destroying fungi aren't the only life forms that may threaten your old-house, for a number of animal species may also find it an attractive host. These include squirrels, chipmunks, rats, raccoons, and porcupines. But the damage these do to a house (although at times severe) is rarely great enough to warrant discussion. Woodpeckers are often considered to be destructive to old-houses, but they really quite blamelessly dig insects out of its woodwork. A farmer friend of mine from upstate New York didn't quite see it in this light when one of these birds began pecking holes in his cedar-shingled roof. He sheepishly admitted that he had opened fire on the hapless woodpecker with a shotgun, putting more holes in his roof than the bird would have in a year.

The insects that the woodpecker was after were the true threat to the farmer's house, for the several species of these that parasitize the old-house rank second only to fungi as the causes of its disease. The extermination of many of these insect pests isn't really a task you should become personally involved with, as it usually requires the use of highly toxic chemicals that aren't even available to you unless you have a pest-control license. You should nonetheless know enough about these parasites to readily identify them and the signs of their presence and to take precautionary measures against their possible tenancy in your old-house.

Termites have an all too well-deserved reputation for being the most destructive of the insects that may parasitize your old-house. Their notoriety is indeed so great they are often given credit for the handiwork of fungi or other less destructive species of insects. I have been summoned to just as many false alarms for the terrible termite as I have for the mysterious and omnipotent dry-rot. But

 Habitat of subterranean termites

Habitat of both subterranean and drywood termites

Termite incidence in the United States

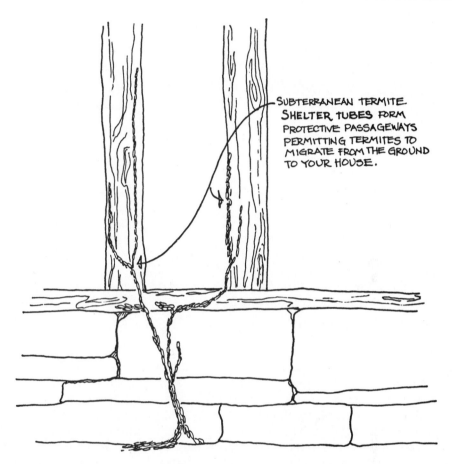

SUBTERRANEAN TERMITE SHELTER TUBES FORM PROTECTIVE PASSAGEWAYS PERMITTING TERMITES TO MIGRATE FROM THE GROUND TO YOUR HOUSE.

the termite is certainly not a mythical creature and within the confines of his environment can pose the most serious of threats to the health of your old-house.

The most numerous species of termite in the United States nests in the ground, leaving it only to feast on your house or another tempting supply of wood and during brief recolonization flights during the first warm spell in the spring (usually just after a rain). These subterranean termites are extremely sensitive to small changes in temperature and humidity and cannot survive for long in an unprotected environment. They consequently construct earthlike shelter tubes whenever it's necessary for them to travel from the ground to a source of wood. These tubes are often found on the inside surface of foundation walls, extending from soil to sill and make the presence of these termites quite evident.

Less common are the dry-wood termites. They have a very limited habitat in this country but can be devastating in the areas in which they thrive. Unlike their earth-bound cousins, they may gain access to your house by simply flying through an open window or vent. They may then eat their way into any exposed woodwork, establishing both their feeding and nesting facilities there.

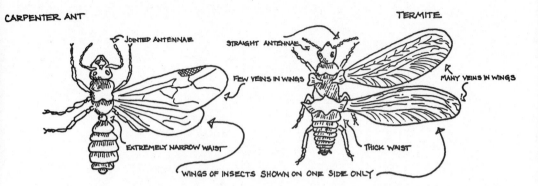

CARPENTER ANT

TERMITE

JOINTED ANTENNAE

STRAIGHT ANTENNAE

FEW VEINS IN WINGS

MANY VEINS IN WINGS

EXTREMELY NARROW WAIST

THICK WAIST

WINGS OF INSECTS SHOWN ON ONE SIDE ONLY

The anatomical differences between carpenter ants and termites

Both subterranean and dry-wood termites have a voracious appetite for wood and can reduce any wooden portion of your house to a hollowed-out shell in a short time. If you find incontrovertible evidence of their presence, don't lose any time in procuring the services of a pest-control operator. If you live within the habitat of the subterranean termite, never leave wood scraps, posts, or concrete forms in contact with the earth for any length of time, for they may attract these termites, which may later spread into your house.

Although often mistaken for termites, carpenter ants have very different physical attributes and don't eat wood but merely make their homes in it. This is why they are seen so much more frequently than termites, as they bustle about in search of the plant and insect secretions that constitute their diet. Carpenter ants have a swarm similar to termites, but this takes place in early summer, rather than during the spring. Their nests aren't particularly large, but they are commonly located in particularly troublesome spots, such as where several timbers are joined together. The ants select these costly-to-repair areas because they have often been previously softened by the attack of fungi attracted by the moisture that often collects in such locations. If you successfully shield the wooden parts of your old-house from moisture, you thus not only protect it against fungi, but from carpenter ants as well.

Carpenter bee

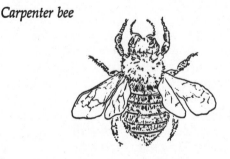

Physical Insect	Nature of Description	Telltale Damage	Signs
y-wood Termites	Swarmers are $1/2''$ to $5/8''$ long and are dark brown to black.	Clean, extensive cavities across the grain.	Mounds of pellets of partially-digested wood and paper; thin brownish-black seals on entrance holes.
oterranean Termites	Swarmers are $1/3''$ to $1/2''$ long and are pale yellow-brown to black in color.	Very extensive galleries excavated with the grain.	Earthlike shelter tubes leading from nest to ground.
rpenter Ant	Males up to $7/16''$ long, winged queens up to $3/4''$ long. Black.	Galleries excavated with the grain, usually not longer than 4' but often where several timbers join together.	Sizable piles of coarse sawdust outside nests. The ants themselves are frequently seen both inside and outside the house.
rpenter Bee	Similar to a bumble-bee, with a blue-black, green, or purple metallic sheen.	Clean holes in dry wood, around $1/2''$ in diameter and from 4" to 12" deep. Such holes are usually made in unpainted cornices and other exterior woodwork.	Damage is directly visible.
obiid Beetle*	Adults are $1/8''$ to $1/4''$ long, reddish-brown to black in color.	Meandering tunnels with and across the grain primarily in sapwood of pine, fir, spruce, and hemlock, but sometimes in hardwoods.	Look for emergence holes a little larger than $1/16''$ in diameter and sawdust compressed into small, granular pellets.
wderpost Beetle*	Adults are $1/8''$ to $1/4''$ long, reddish-brown to black in color.	Meandering tunnels with and across the grain, only in sapwood of certain species of hardwoods (including oak, ash, and maple).	Look for emergence holes of $1/16''$ in diameter in conjunction with fine, floury sawdust.
l-House Borer*	Adult is $5/8''$ to 1" long, brownish-black in color.	Meandering tunnels with and across the grain in sapwood of pine, spruce, hemlock, and fir.	Look for emergence holes of $1/4''$ diameter and piles of fine, floury sawdust.

ese three species are usually grouped together by pest control operators as owderpost Beetles."

A lesser known and less destructive member of the woodworking industry is the carpenter bee, the females of which may bore deep holes in unpainted woodwork to serve as nests for their families. These excavations are usually from four to twelve inches deep (although the record depth for a carpenter bee nesting

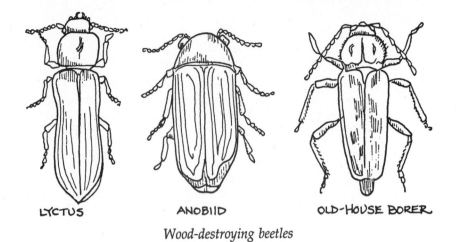

LYCTUS   ANOBIID   OLD-HOUSE BORER

Wood-destroying beetles

hole is ten feet). The holes are drilled at the rate of about one-sixth of an inch per day.

The many species of wood-destroying beetles taken collectively rank second only to the termite in terms of overall destructiveness. These include powderpost beetles, old-house borers, and anobiid beetles, all of which have the same life cycle. The adult female lays eggs in wood that then hatch into larva and tunnel through the wood for from three to twelve years. They then pass through a brief pupal stage before emerging as adult beetles, which mate and begin the cycle once again. The beetles are abroad for one or two weeks in spring or early summer, but as this is such a small fraction of their life span, it's unlikely you'll ever see them.

The larva of powderpost beetles may be brought into your house in pieces of antique furniture or well-seasoned hardwood lumber and may migrate from there into hardwood floors and woodwork. Old-house borers and anobiid beetles usually confine their attacks to the sills, joists, and subflooring of your old-house.

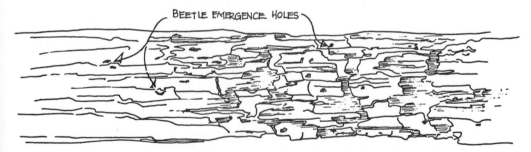

BEETLE EMERGENCE HOLES

THIS WOOD IS AFFLICTED WITH BOTH FUNGAL DECAY AND WOOD DESTROYING BEETLES

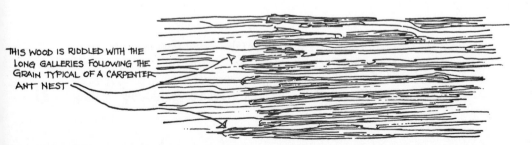

THIS WOOD IS RIDDLED WITH THE LONG GALLERIES FOLLOWING THE GRAIN TYPICAL OF A CARPENTER ANT NEST

The attacks of all of these beetles may be discouraged by promoting good ventilation and hence low moisture content in the wooden parts of your house.

One of the anobiids is the well-known death-watch beetle, which call for their mates in the spring in an unusual and eerie manner. They produce a series of ticks by knocking their heads against a piece of wood. If these love calls are successful, they will be echoed by other beetles. This mysterious ticking, issuing from behind the wall or under the floor of an old-house, was long ago considered an omen of certain death for someone in the household. Although I can see no reason why it should portend death for any *person*, there is justification for them to be thought of as such a portent for the old-house itself. If you see or hear evidence of any of these beetles, it would once again be wise to lose no time in contacting a pest control operator.

CHAPTER

4

The Skeleton
of the Old-House

The Anatomy of the Old-House Skeleton

Nowhere is the similarity between the anatomies of the human being and the old-house more apparent than in their respective skeletons, or frames. All old-houses are sustained by a system of wooden bones and joints that determine their outward form and upon which their inner and outer skins may be fastened. As roofs and floors almost always have a wooden frame, this holds true even in the case of those buildings constructed primarily of brick or stone.

Brick has been a popular American building material since 1615, particularly in the early English settlements in Virginia and the Dutch colonies in New York state. Early bricks weren't hard-baked like modern ones and varied considerably in size and color. New bricks consequently stand out conspicuously in old walls and should therefore never be used for patching old brickwork, where only genuinely old bricks or handmade reproductions will blend harmoniously.

A structural brick wall (one that actually supports the weight of a building— not the thin, decorative veneer to be found on many recent dwellings) must be at least 8″ thick. This thickness is achieved by laying up a double wall of 4″-wide bricks called stretchers, tied together at specified intervals by headers, which are bricks laid at right angles to the wall. The pattern formed by headers and stretchers is known as the bond of the wall, and it provides a useful if not infallible guide to the age of the brickwork.

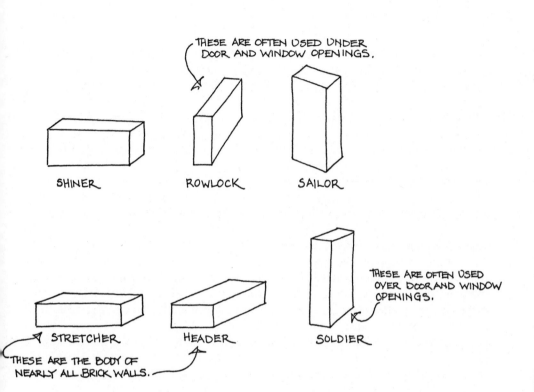

THESE ARE OFTEN USED UNDER DOOR AND WINDOW OPENINGS.

SHINER

ROWLOCK

SAILOR

STRETCHER

HEADER

SOLDIER

THESE ARE OFTEN USED OVER DOOR AND WINDOW OPENINGS.

THESE ARE THE BODY OF NEARLY ALL BRICK WALLS.

Bricks have different names depending on how they are laid in a wall. And walls have different bonds depending on how stretchers and headers are laid in them.

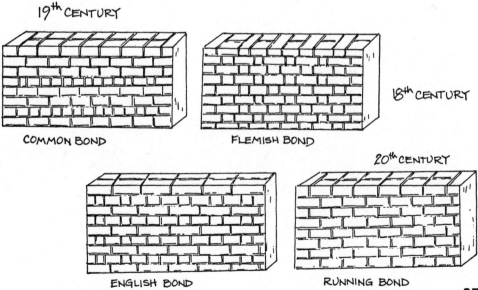

19th CENTURY

COMMON BOND

FLEMISH BOND

18th CENTURY

ENGLISH BOND

20th CENTURY

RUNNING BOND

35

Flemish bond was commonly used in wall construction during the 18th century, in conjunction with English bond in the foundations. These had largely given way to the simpler American, or common, bond by the middle of the following century, which was itself superseded by running bond in the early 1900s (this has no headers at all, but in their place utilizes metal wall ties).

Stone has also been a popular building material since the early days of the colonies, having been a favorite of the Pennsylvania Dutch, Flemish, and French Huguenot settlers. Limestone, sandstone, granite, and marble have all been commonly used in American old-houses—the variety selected usually depending on the proximity of the quarries to the building site (the weightiness of stone makes it very expensive to transport). The once popular brownstone and bluestone, although often considered separate species of stone, are actually just particular colorations of sandstone.

Structural stone walls were generally much thicker than their brick counterparts, ranging from one and a half to three feet and more in thickness—the thicker the wall, the earlier the house. Many 19th-century buildings, such as the famous urban brownstones, seemingly of massive masonry construction, in reality have but a thin veneer of stone over their skeletons.

Some old stone walls are *dry-laid* without mortar of any kind. Such masonry is strong and long lasting if their mason took care to observe the following rules: (1) Each stone should rest on *two* of its fellows; (2) vertical joints in adjacent courses should never line up with each other; and (3) the wall should be slightly thicker at its base than at its top.

A dry-laid wall actually has two distinct advantages over one constructed with mortar. If above ground, the interstices between stones permit all-important ventilation, thereby discouraging fungi and insects from destroying wooden portions of the house. If below ground, the same spaces allow water to drain freely through the wall, preventing the build-up of hydrostatic pressure that would inevitably crack an impermeable surface.

Most masonry walls of old-houses nevertheless employ mortar as a bonding and leveling agent between bricks or stones. The first American mortar was probably made of mud or clay, strengthened with straw or hog's hair. This lost favor during the 18th century to a lime mortar made (in coastal areas) of crushed oyster shells, which was used until the discovery of natural hydraulic cement (pulverized limestone) in 1819. This in turn was almost universally used until the first U.S. patent for portland cement was granted in 1871. This artificial combination of lime, sili-

NOTE THAT JOINTS DON'T LINE UP ONE ABOVE THE OTHER

A well-constructed dry-laid stone wall

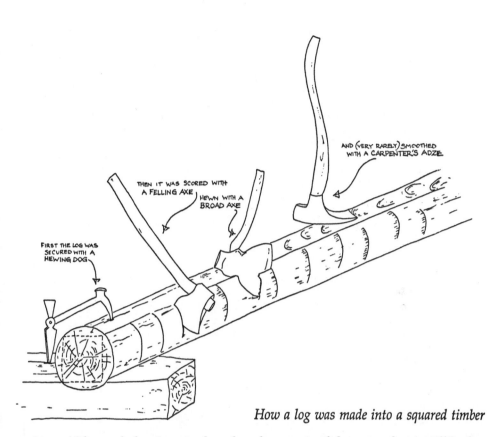

AND (VERY RARELY) SMOOTHED
WITH A CARPENTER'S ADZE.

THEN IT WAS SCORED WITH
A FELLING AXE

HEWN WITH A
BROAD AXE

FIRST THE LOG WAS
SECURED WITH A
HEWING DOG.

How a log was made into a squared timber

ca, iron oxide, and alumina produced such a successful mortar that it still is the active ingredient in the billions of yards of concrete poured every year in the United States.

Wood has nonetheless been the most popular building material since earliest colonial times. Most of the first settlers were English and brought with them from the mother country a penchant for homes framed with heavy oak beams. Since the New World was blessed with seemingly limitless stands of timber, the English braced frame house emigrated with the American colonists. As oak wasn't always available, such other native woods as white and yellow pine, poplar, hemlock, and chestnut were sometimes used in its place.

The timbers used in the construction of a braced frame house were invariably hewn (that is, squared with an axe) from logs blocked up off the ground and secured to the block with hewing dogs. After chalk lines were snapped on each side of the log, the carpenter (or joiner as he was called in those days) would walk astride the log from end to end, making diagonal cuts to and perhaps a little past the lines with an ordinary axe.

He then exchanged his axe for a broad axe, a tool with a short crooked handle and a single-beveled blade of great width. With this he would slice off the previously scored portion of the log. When he had thus hewn to the two lines, the log would be rotated 90°, and a new line would be struck to which he would likewise hew.

37

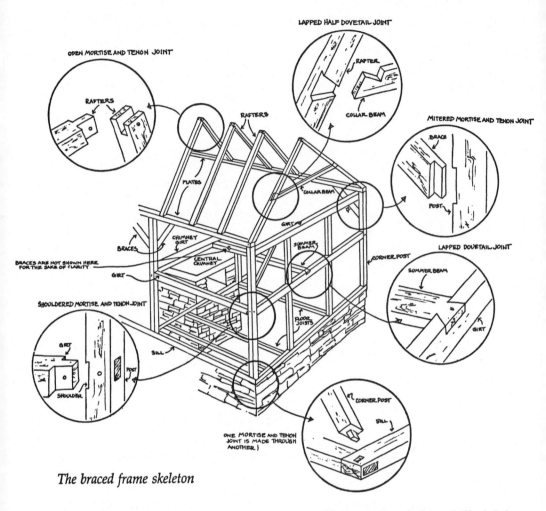

OPEN MORTISE AND TENON JOINT

RAFTERS

LAPPED HALF DOVETAIL JOINT

RAFTER

COLLAR BEAM

MITERED MORTISE AND TENON JOINT

BRACE

POST

RAFTERS

PLATES

COLLAR BEAM

GIRT

CHIMNEY GIRT

BRACES

CENTRAL CHIMNEY

SUMMER BEAM

CORNER POST

BRACES ARE NOT SHOWN HERE FOR THE SAKE OF CLARITY

GIRT

LAPPED DOVETAIL JOINT

SOMMER BEAM

SHOULDERED MORTISE AND TENON JOINT

GIRT

SILL

POST

SHOULDER

FLOOR JOISTS

GIRT

CORNER POST

SILL

ONE MORTISE AND TENON JOINT IS MADE THROUGH ANOTHER !

The braced frame skeleton

The braced frame house

The result of this skilled labor would be the hand-hewn timbers to be seen in most of our early houses and barns, characterized by the shallow diagonal slashes made by the axe in the first stage of hewing. It's a common misconception that timbers were hewn with another tool known as an adze, which was only occasionally employed by joiners to smooth beams that had already been hewn.

After all the timbers for the frame of a house had been hewn, they would be cut to exact length and marked for the mortise-and-tenon joints, which would soon lock them together. Each of these incredibly strong joints consists of a rectangular hole (mortise) in one timber into which an exactly corresponding protrusion on another timber's end (tenon) is fastened by an oak peg, or treenail (pronounced "trunnel"), which has been driven through a hole previously bored through the joint. The tenons would then be laboriously sawn and the mortises meticulously excavated with auger and chisel.

The first step in putting the frame together was to lay the heavy sills, or bottommost timbers on the foundation, with their ends mortised and tenoned together. A pair of soon-to-be vertical timbers, or posts, would next be joined by a single transverse member known as a girt, forming the configuration of the letter H known as a bent. This unit was then raised into an erect position by a number of people manning long poles and blocks and tackle. (It wasn't uncommon for neighbors and friends to show up for a large house or barn raising.)

This procedure was now repeated for as many bents (commonly four) as it took to complete the frame. After they were all erected and temporarily held in place, the topmost horizontal timbers, or plates, were lowered onto the tenons that had been fashioned on the tops of the posts. As this was being accomplished, the diagonal braces running from post to plate were inserted into their respective mortises. Once the plates were pinned to the posts, the rafters, or roof timbers, were raised and floor joists (often rough logs with but their top surface hewn) were laid, completing the skeleton. (Small-dimensioned "studs" were used as nailers for inner and outer wall surfaces between posts, but as these weren't structural, they weren't really part of the skeleton as they were later to become in the balloon frame.)

The braced frame was extremely strong, but required much time and skill to fabricate and imposed severe restrictions on the form of the building it supported. It was nevertheless more practical until around 1825 to hew large timbers at the building site, than to transport them to and from a distant and rudimentary sawmill. Between that time and 1840, however, countless sawmills utilizing the newly invented circular saw sprang into existence (earlier mills had up-and-down saws). The capacity of these mills to produce copious and easily procurable quantities of accurately dimensioned lumber and small timber opened the door to a revolutionary change in building construction.

The first man to walk through that door was a Chicago businessman named George Washington Snow, who constructed his warehouse in 1832 with a radically different skeleton which he called a balloon frame. This was made of far lighter timbers than would be called for by a braced frame. They were no longer mortised and tenoned together but now fastened with cut nails. (The recent invention of these economical fasteners contributed greatly to the balloon frame success.)

The new skeleton's lack of reliance on heavy timbers and mortised and tenoned braces made possible a flexibility of form impossible in the old framing style. The balloon frame thus paved the way for the incredible architectural variety of the last half of the 19th century. Windows and doors could now be located more freely, and houses sprouted conical turrets, octagonal towers, and any other whims their architects might devise.

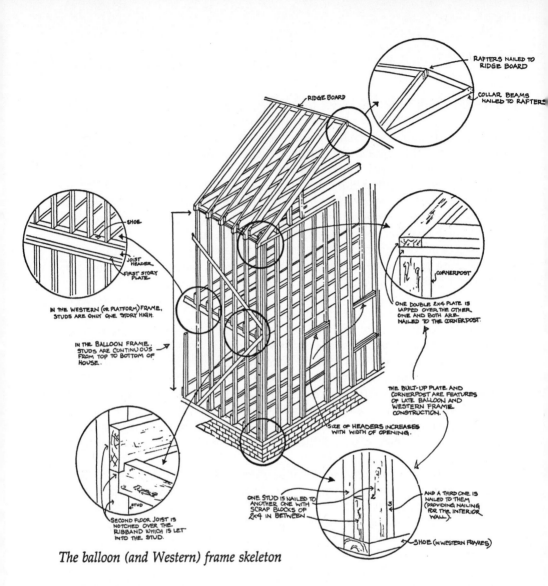

RIDGE BOARD

RAFTERS NAILED TO RIDGE BOARD

COLLAR BEAMS NAILED TO RAFTERS

SHOE

JOIST HEADER

FIRST STORY PLATE

IN THE WESTERN (OR PLATFORM) FRAME, STUDS ARE ONLY ONE STORY HIGH.

IN THE BALLOON FRAME, STUDS ARE CONTINUOUS FROM TOP TO BOTTOM OF HOUSE.

CORNERPOST

ONE DOUBLE 2x4 PLATE IS LAPPED OVER THE OTHER ONE AND BOTH ARE NAILED TO THE CORNERPOST.

THE BUILT-UP PLATE AND CORNERPOST ARE FEATURES OF LATE BALLOON AND WESTERN FRAME CONSTRUCTION.

SIZE OF HEADERS INCREASES WITH WIDTH OF OPENING.

STUD

SECOND FLOOR JOIST IS NOTCHED OVER THE RIBBAND WHICH IS LET INTO THE STUD.

ONE STUD IS NAILED TO ANOTHER ONE WITH SCRAP BLOCKS OF 2x4 IN BETWEEN

3

AND A THIRD ONE IS NAILED TO THEM (PROVIDING NAILING FOR THE INTERIOR WALL).

SHOE (IN WESTERN FRAMES)

The balloon (and Western) frame skeleton

Although barns and outbuildings were often constructed in the old manner until the early 1900s, the balloon frame was almost exclusively used in residential construction after about 1850. By the middle of the 20th century, however, it had been replaced with a variant style known as the Western, or platform, frame. This differs in only one important respect from its predecessor: the studs, or vertical framing members, in a balloon frame always extend continuously from sill to plate, whereas in the platform system they are but one story high.

The balloon frame house

Skeletal Surgery and Chiropractic:
Repairing and Straightening the Frame

Regardless of the type of skeleton that supports your old-house, it may have grown diseased or deformed with age and infirmity. Its bones and joints may be infected with fungus, infested with insect parasites, or may have lost their original *truth*. (A frame is said to be true when its sills, plates, and ridge are level and straight and its posts or studs are plumb, or vertical.) An old-house with a crooked frame may appear picturesque, but it may be on the road to total collapse.

In order to arrive at an accurate diagnosis of the condition of your old-house's frame, it's necessary to give it a thorough physical examination. Penetrate the darkest corners of attic and cellar with a strong flashlight and pocketknife, studying and probing the frame for indications of the presence of termites, carpenter ants, beetles, or fungi. Look the house over for outward signs of an untrue frame, such as out-of-level floors, bulging walls, and sagging ridges.

If your eye tells you that the frame may be out of truth, you should examine it more closely with the aid of three tools unique in their simplicity, economy, and incredible accuracy. The first of these is nothing more than a length of mason's twine, with which you may easily assess the straightness of a ridge, plate, or post by holding it taut alongside them, thereby creating a mathematically straight line with which to compare them. The second tool is the plumb bob, which is merely a pointed weight hung at the end of another piece of twine, together creating a tangible arrow showing the direction of the earth's gravitational force. The plumbness of a post or stud is easily ascertained when compared with such an arrow.

The third tool is the water level, easily made from an ordinary garden hose by

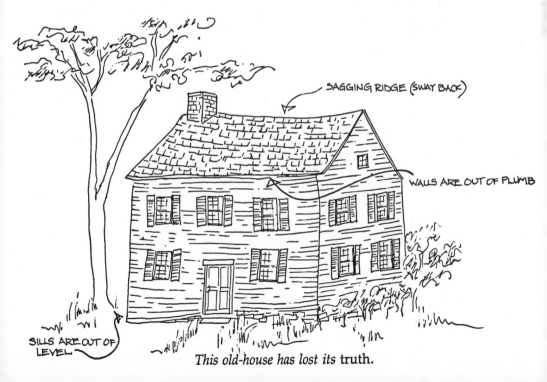

SAGGING RIDGE (SWAY BACK)

WALLS ARE OUT OF PLUMB

SILLS ARE OUT OF LEVEL

This old-house has lost its truth.

adding two foot-long clear plastic extensions fitted with hose caps to each of its ends. When you have filled this remarkable instrument with water, you may use it to determine accurately the relative heights of points separated by considerable distances or obstacles, even when they are out of sight of each other. It is thus invaluable in comparing the level of a floor or sill at one end of a house with that at the other.

The almost magical performance of the water level is entirely due to the well-known yet extraordinary capacity of water to seek its own level. Hold one of the ends of the water-filled hose in each hand (with hose caps removed, for these are only to prevent spillage when moving around and prevent proper functioning of the level). The water will rise to precisely the same level in each end of the hose. If you now slowly move one hand higher than the other, the water will fall in that end of the hose while it rises in the other until the two find their own level again. They will infallibly do so, despite the convolutions of the intervening hose (it might for instance pass over the roof of your house!), unless it hasn't been adequately filled and contains air bubbles. If you suspect this to be the case, reconnect the hose to your water supply and let it run until no more bubbles appear at the other end.

If the floors of your old-house are so out of level that beds and tables require stacks of books under one or more of their legs to render them reasonably horizontal, you should make a water level map of the premises. To do so, begin by choosing a datum point to which your measurements may refer. The fireplace hearth is good for this, as it's unlikely to have moved much from its original position; but any point will do. While a helper holds one end of the water level at a convenient height off the floor at this point, you may move around the house with the other end, taking readings at various locations, including every corner. Compare the height of the top of the water column off the floor at one end of the hose with that at the other at each of these points and record the difference on your map. (If the height of the column is for example 38" above the hearth and 46"

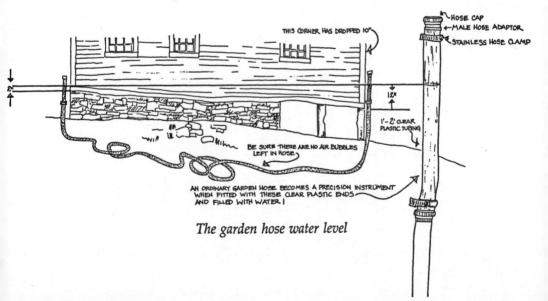

THIS CORNER HAS DROPPED 10"

HOSE CAP
MALE HOSE ADAPTOR
STAINLESS HOSE CLAMP

12"

1'–2' CLEAR PLASTIC TUBING

BE SURE THERE ARE NO AIR BUBBLES LEFT IN HOSE.

AN ORDINARY GARDEN HOSE BECOMES A PRECISION INSTRUMENT WHEN FITTED WITH THESE CLEAR PLASTIC ENDS AND FILLED WITH WATER!

The garden hose water level

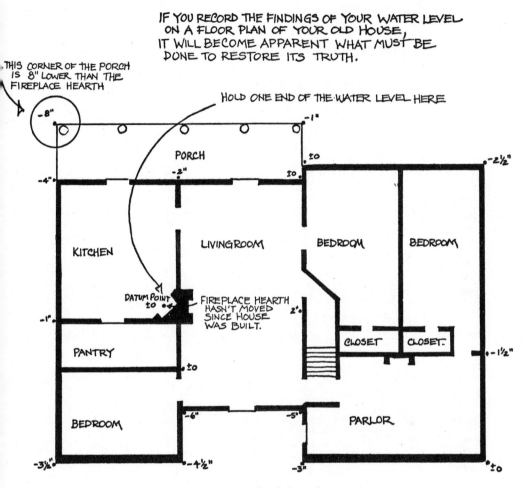

IF YOU RECORD THE FINDINGS OF YOUR WATER LEVEL ON A FLOOR PLAN OF YOUR OLD HOUSE, IT WILL BECOME APPARENT WHAT MUST BE DONE TO RESTORE ITS TRUTH.

THIS CORNER OF THE PORCH IS 8" LOWER THAN THE FIREPLACE HEARTH

−8"

HOLD ONE END OF THE WATER LEVEL HERE

−1"

±0

−2½"

PORCH

−2"

±0

−4"

KITCHEN

LIVINGROOM

BEDROOM

BEDROOM

DATUM POINT ±0

FIREPLACE HEARTH HASN'T MOVED SINCE HOUSE WAS BUILT.

2"

−1"

PANTRY

CLOSET

CLOSET

−1½"

±0

BEDROOM

−6"

−5"

PARLOR

−3½"

−4½"

−3"

±0

A water level "map"

above the floor at one corner of the house, that corner has settled 8". Record this as −8" on the map.)

When you've completed such a map, you may easily determine which parts of your old-house need to be raised (or, rarely, lowered) to restore its floors to their original level (differences of an inch or less usually aren't worth worrying about). You are now in a position to evaluate the combined testimony of the mason's twine, plumb bob, water level, and your explorations with pocketknife and flashlight. The frame of your old-house may be nearly true, yet portions may be rotten and need replacement or it might be completely sound, but out of truth. It's more likely that it will be suffering from both maladies simultaneously, thus requiring the services of both old-house chiropractor and surgeon.

It's usually far better to restore the frame of your old-house to a reasonable facsimile of truth before attempting to repair its rotten or infested members. You should by now be well aware of whether or not its ridge is sagging, plates bowed, posts out of plumb, or sills out of level. It now only remains for you to reverse the

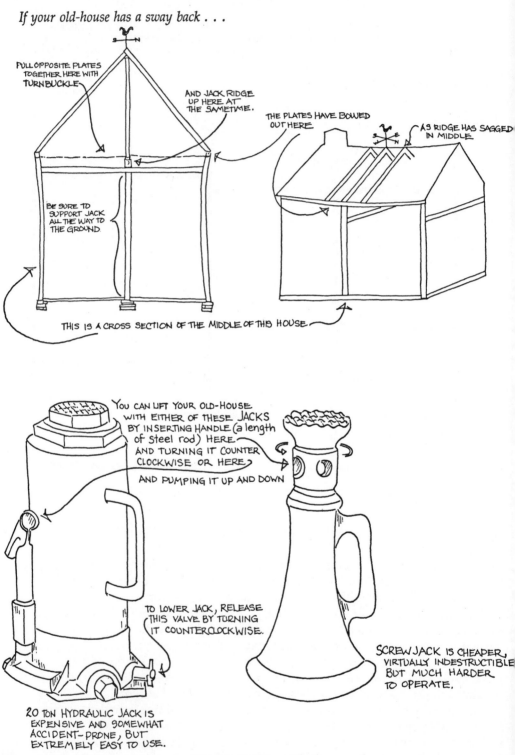

If your old-house has a sway back . . .

PULL OPPOSITE PLATES TOGETHER HERE WITH TURNBUCKLE.

AND JACK RIDGE UP HERE AT THE SAME TIME.

THE PLATES HAVE BOWED OUT HERE

AS RIDGE HAS SAGGED IN MIDDLE

BE SURE TO SUPPORT JACK ALL THE WAY TO THE GROUND.

THIS IS A CROSS SECTION OF THE MIDDLE OF THIS HOUSE.

YOU CAN LIFT YOUR OLD-HOUSE WITH EITHER OF THESE JACKS BY INSERTING HANDLE (a length of steel rod) HERE. AND TURNING IT COUNTER CLOCKWISE OR HERE. AND PUMPING IT UP AND DOWN

TO LOWER JACK, RELEASE THIS VALVE BY TURNING IT COUNTERCLOCKWISE.

SCREW JACK IS CHEAPER, VIRTUALLY INDESTRUCTIBLE BUT MUCH HARDER TO OPERATE.

20 TON HYDRAULIC JACK IS EXPENSIVE AND SOMEWHAT ACCIDENT-PRONE, BUT EXTREMELY EASY TO USE.

Two kinds of house jack

process that caused it to lose its truth. It's important to think this through very carefully before actually beginning to true the frame.

One of the commonest deformations of the old-house skeleton is the sway-back syndrome, in which the thrust of the roof causes both plates to bow outward at their centers, thus allowing the rafters to move down and out and the middle of the ridge consequently to drop. In order to reverse this process, you must simultaneously lift the center of the ridge and pull the plates together at their midpoints. Your old-house frame may have a completely different malady, but you may still use the same type of analysis on its particular complaint. In order to restore it to truth, you must determine what combination of forces acted on it to cause the present distortion and what must be done to reverse that process.

It now only remains for you to physically implement your plan. You now know exactly *where* you want to move your old-house's frame, but *how* can you lift or pull something as big and heavy as a house? This really isn't as formidable a task as it might appear, once you're equipped with the right tools for the job—the most indispensable of which are several house jacks (don't use automobile jacks unless they're designed for heavy trucks).

You may use either hydraulic or screw jacks to move your house, the first

In order to lift a very heavy load . . .

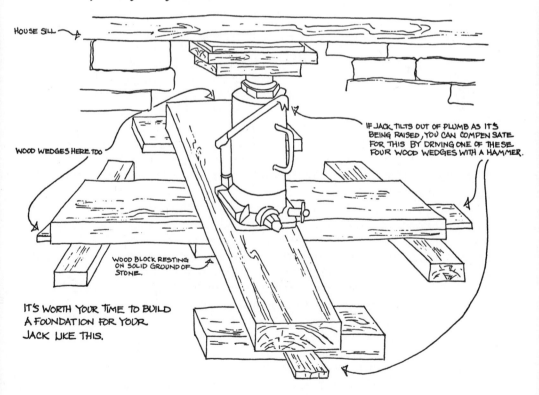

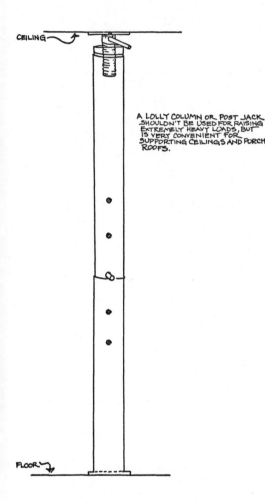

CEILING

A LOLLY COLUMN OR POST JACK SHOULDN'T BE USED FOR RAISING EXTREMELY HEAVY LOADS, BUT IS VERY CONVENIENT FOR SUPPORTING CEILINGS AND PORCH ROOFS.

FLOOR

being by far the quickest and most convenient, but also the most expensive and easily damaged. I recommend for this reason that you rent hydraulic jacks or buy used screw jacks. The lifting capacity of a jack is determined by the diameter and length of its threads (a screw jack with threads 2" in diameter and 12" long will safely lift 15 tons as much as one foot). It's impossible to advise you what rating a jack should have for your particular project, but it should be somewhere between 8 and 20 tons, depending on the size and construction of your house. (If in doubt, play it safe and use a heavier jack than you think you need.)

No matter which type of jacks you use, it's essential that they remain perfectly plumb while they are lifting your old-house. Once one begins to get out of plumb, it will rapidly become more and more so as more pressure is brought to bear on it. If this process is allowed to continue, the jack will suddenly lose its load altogether—an occurrence that could be very dangerous to your house and yourself. As a jack always exerts equal upward and downward force, you must therefore be sure to provide it with a solid and level base. If the load you're lifting isn't that heavy, you can just use a 1' square of 2"-thick lumber, but if it's substantial it's well worth while constructing a more elaborate base.

One special kind of screw jack deserves brief mention, even though it's unlikely to help you to true your frame. This is the post jack, or Lally column, a relatively light-duty jack used far more to support static loads (often a girder supporting first floor joists) than to provide motive power. Since their height is telescopically adjustable from about 4' to 8', they may nevertheless be of great use in supporting ceilings and porches during rehabilitation.

The house jack is capable of pushing an old-house with great force, but you may also need a tool that can pull it with equal power. The ingenious pulling tool known by its trade name as the Come-Along is extremely convenient to operate, but isn't always powerful enough for this purpose. I once utilized a winch mounted on a jeep to pull a dislocated beam into position, but Jeeps and winches aren't always available. The most versatile, inexpensive, and powerful tools for

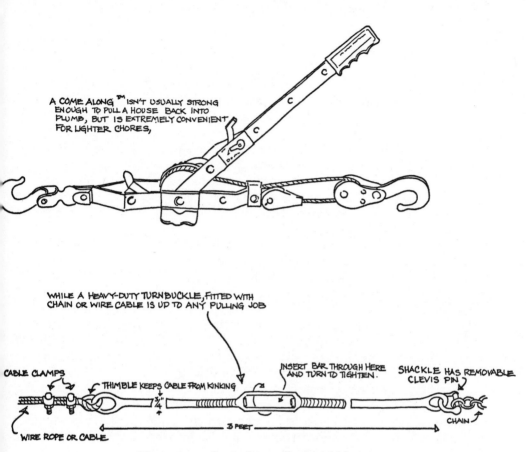

A COME ALONG ™ ISN'T USUALLY STRONG ENOUGH TO PULL A HOUSE BACK INTO PLUMB, BUT IS EXTREMELY CONVENIENT FOR LIGHTER CHORES,

WHILE A HEAVY-DUTY TURNBUCKLE, FITTED WITH CHAIN OR WIRE CABLE IS UP TO ANY PULLING JOB

CABLE CLAMPS

THIMBLE KEEPS CABLE FROM KINKING

INSERT BAR THROUGH HERE AND TURN TO TIGHTEN.

SHACKLE HAS REMOVABLE CLEVIS PIN

$\frac{3}{4}''$

3 FEET

CHAIN

WIRE ROPE OR CABLE

You may need a tool to pull your old-house . . .

the job are common turnbuckles, although they must be of impressive dimensions (mine are 5' long and 1" in diameter).

If your old-house has the sway-back syndrome, you may profitably employ such a turnbuckle to pull its opposing plates or posts together, while simultaneously pushing the sag out of its ridge with a house jack. The turnbuckle should be located midway between them and should be secured with chain or wire cable (rope stretches too much). Before making the final attachments, make sure the turnbuckle is extended to its maximum length and that you've taken all the slack out of the chain or cable (if you don't, you'll run out of threads on the turnbuckle long before you begin to move your house). Once you've inserted bars through each of the turnbuckle's two eyes and have these securely wedged or held (in order to keep the chain or cable from twisting), you may insert a third bar through its center and pull your house together.

Now that you have brought the frame of your old-house back into truth, there may still be diseased portions of it that should be cut out and replaced. The exact nature of this surgery is determined by the extent of the decay or insect damage and the function of the afflicted members. If a sill, post, or plate is totally destroyed, it obviously will have to be replaced in its entirety, ideally with an identical transplant (see Appendix). Yet this often isn't the case, for old-house **47** disease doesn't always destroy a complete framing member before it goes on to another but will commonly afflict portions of several simultaneously. There are three approaches to strengthening a partially diseased member: scabbing, sistering, and scarfing.

The first of these is by far the easiest, but the weakest of the three. It merely consists of nailing a scab, or short board, alongside the diseased area, but can be a valid repair—provided not much strength is required of it. If a framing member has only been superficially damaged and retains sufficient structural strength, a piece may thus be scabbed beside it in order to provide a good nailing surface for a wall, ceiling, or floor.

Sistering is really a term used more by boatbuilders than carpenters, although the technique is shared in common. A sister is a full-sized member fastened alongside a diseased one, thus restoring and somewhat adding to its original strength, without necessitating the difficulty of removing the partially damaged piece in its entirety. It's nevertheless advisable when sistering or scabbing to cut away any material actually infected or infested in order to prevent the original malady from spreading. The shortcoming of both techniques is that, despite the removal of this material, the joint between the two members may accumulate moisture and hence promote a new cycle of disease.

Scarfing is much more time-consuming than scabbing or sistering, but it is a strong and elegant technique that may be viewed with pleasure. There are many different kinds of scarf joints, depending on the particular type of strength required of them but all permit you to repair a diseased member without sisters or scabs.

Compression scarf joints are relatively easy to cut, usually involving nothing more than a simple lap joint (sometimes mitred or cut at 45°), but simple tension and tension and bending joints are more elaborate and consequently more time-consuming to effect. The considerable effort you might expend in making this last joint could nevertheless be worth while if only the last few feet of a long beam were decayed and the ceiling and floor fastened to it were in good shape. As you would have to remove both of these to effect a total replacement of the beam or to sister it (scabbing wouldn't be a strong enough solution to consider), a tension and bending scarf joint might actually prove the easiest alternative.

There are times when a partially diseased framing member may be suitably and far more easily repaired with steel rather than wood. Angle irons, U channels, and plate steel of ¼" or more in thickness may be ordered from steel fabricators precut and drilled to your specifications. These may then be used to reinforce

THIS JOINT MAY ACCUMULATE MOISTURE WHICH WOULD PROMOTE FURTHER DECAY.

Sistering a decayed joist

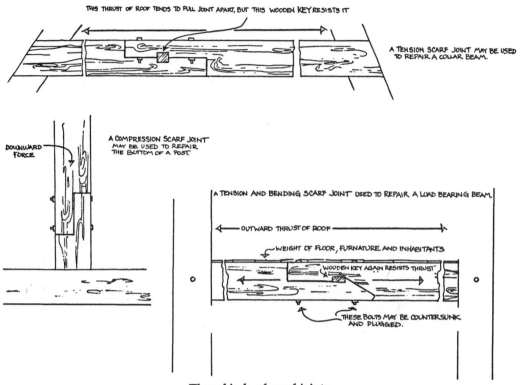

Three kinds of scarf joints

weakened members that would be difficult to repair with wood and aren't subject to the closest scrutiny. A steel plate may thus be screwed or bolted to the entire length of a partially decayed beam, forming an extremely strong, yet thin sister or a piece of this plate may be bent into a U shape and used to reinforce a weakened mortise and tenon joint between a post and beam.

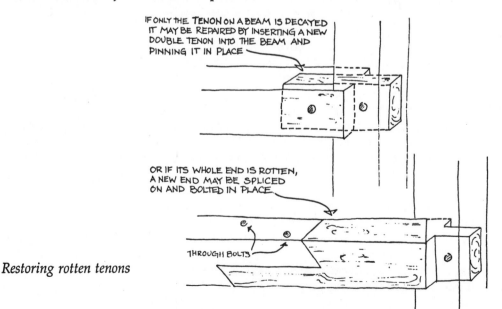

Restoring rotten tenons

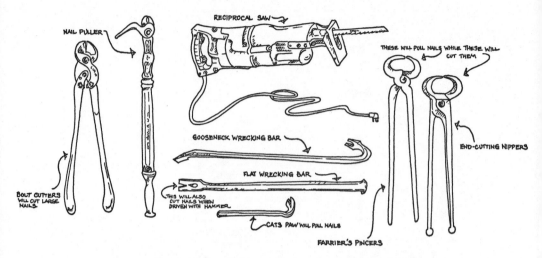

Some of the old-house surgeon's most useful tools

One of the easiest ways to tell how much experience an old-house surgeon has is to observe the manner in which they remove partially diseased wood and in particular how they extract the multitudinous nails that may secure it. If the process is lengthy, the surgeon exasperated, and good material is split and gouged along with the bad, they are undoubtedly new to the field. You shouldn't rely on the claw on your hammer to remove nails (although it can at times be the best tool for the job), but should have at your disposal several other relatively inexpensive tools for the purpose. A flat and gooseneck wrecking bar, catspaw, nail-puller and *farrier's (horse-shoer's) pincers* are indispensable devices for extracting nails in different circumstances. There are also times when it's more expedient to cut a nail than to pull it, for which purpose the end of a good quality flat wrecking bar (when driven with a hammer) or a pair of bolt-cutters or end-cutting nippers will prove invaluable.

Once the nails have been cut or removed from a piece of wood, it still will very likely have to be cut before it may be removed. As indispensable as a Skilsaw is for most work, this is one place it isn't usually that useful. Bad wood may usually be more easily cut out and subdivided into smaller, more conveniently handled sections with a small chainsaw or a Sawzall (reciprocal saw).

I once was apprenticed to a seventy-year-old carpenter on Nantucket Island who strongly impressed me with the extreme usefulness of a sharp handsaw and chisel for this purpose. He kept all his hand tools with cutting edges scalpel-sharp. If the slightest nick developed in an edge, he would drop whatever he was doing and rush for his file or whetstone. With such well-honed tools, he could make astonishingly quick and accurate cuts in the most awkward positions imaginable. He nevertheless cursed and screamed at his Skilsaw (on the rare occasions he used it), oblivious of the fact that it too required sharpening. Yet he was a superb old-time craftsman despite this lapse and taught me that the lowly chisel and handsaw (if kept meticulously honed and filed) were capable of almost miraculous old-house surgery.

5

The Hair and Scalp: The Roof and Its Coverings

The roofs of many of the very first American dwellings were thatched with straw or reeds—a cheap, warm and attractive covering to protect their otherwise bald heads from the vagaries of the weather. Certainly no other roof covering has ever been devised that more closely resembles a head of human hair! Thatched roofs nonetheless never gained the popularity in North America that they had in England, for the climate proved too extreme for them to last long and the colonists were too concerned at their inherent fire hazard.

The abundant stands of prime white pine and cedar made shingles manufactured from these woods the logical successor to thatch as a roofing material. These shingles were far more durable than thatch and were far less of a fire hazard. Pine or cedar logs were squared and cut into 2' sections called bolts, from which shingles were riven, or split, by striking a heavy knifelike tool known as a froe with a wooden maul or club. The roughly shaped shingles were then clamped in a wooden shingle-horse and carefully shaved to a taper with a drawknife.

In an extremely mistaken attempt at historical authenticity, many "restorers" of old-houses will use the more costly "hand-split" shakes instead of shingles. These are thick, irregular and have no taper, closely resembling old-time shingles as they came straight from the froe. Few craftsmen in years gone by would have considered shingling a roof with such rough, unfinished specimens as these (unless it was on a shed or barn).

A machine was devised toward the middle of the 19th century capable of **51** sawing tapered shingles far more rapidly than they could ever be split and dressed. Sawn shingles are still produced today by similar machines and don't differ greatly in appearance from those dressed with a drawknife (particularly after they have weathered on the roof for a few years). A roof laid with such shingles will be tighter, cheaper, and far more authentic than one shingled with shakes.

Slate shingles achieved great popularity in certain areas of the country, due to their fire resistance, aesthetic appeal, and extremely long life. They became available during the 19th century in several colors and shapes, which were often combined on the same roof, creating a highly ornamental effect. If it weren't for their costliness and great weight, these shingles would undoubtedly have become the favorite American roof covering. Due to these shortcomings, their use was restricted to areas relatively near slate quarries and to especially heavily framed roofs that were able to accommodate their weight.

Ceramic tiles were also used to shingle roofs from early colonial times to about 1830, at which time they unaccountably passed out of favor. They were considerably lighter and cheaper than slate and were produced in both flat and

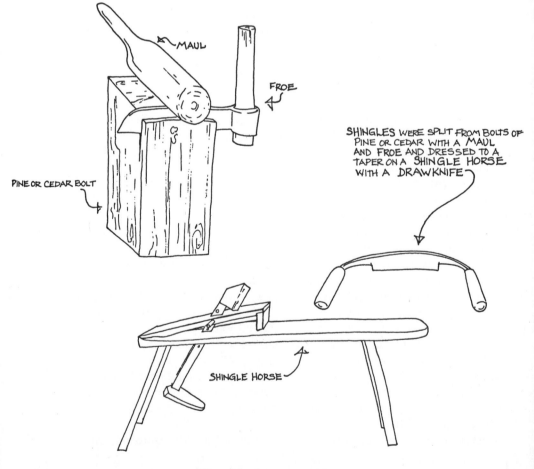

How shingles were made

semicylindrical configurations. Although still popular in tropical and semitropical climates, ceramic roof tiles have been used but infrequently in the North after 1830, with the exception of a brief flurry of popularity during the vogue of the "Spanish style" in the early 20th century.

Copper, galvanized iron, zinc, and terne were also common roofing materials in America, with terne, commonly known as tin, undoubtedly proving most popular (particularly in the late 19th century). Terne is sheet iron coated with an equal mixture of tin and lead, the thickness of this coating determining both its cost and longevity. This fine roofing material is still available today in weights of from 8 to 40 pounds [the weight of terne is determined by the weight of its tin-lead coating per square (100 ft^2)], although you may have to be persistent to find a hardware or building supply dealer who carries it.

Terne roofs are extremely long-lasting when they are regularly painted. It's not at all unusual to see these red, green, or black roofs still in use after nearly a century. Some of them are composed of relatively small pieces of metal soldered together on all sides but most employ a standing seam (an ingenious locking and leakproof joint) between sheets of terne.

Composition roofing was developed during the mid-19th century to fill the need for a leakproof covering for the flat roofs then becoming popular on urban buildings. The composition material (pieces of cloth, felt, or paper soaked in tar) had the advantage of being manufactured in large sheets or rolls, which meant fewer seams for water to seep through. The built-up roof of today (used on flat roofs or those with very slight pitches) is essentially the same, being composed of five alternating layers of tar and composition roofing.

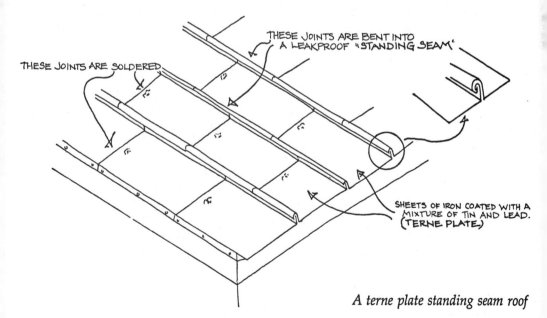

THESE JOINTS ARE BENT INTO A LEAKPROOF "STANDING SEAM"

THESE JOINTS ARE SOLDERED.

SHEETS OF IRON COATED WITH A MIXTURE OF TIN AND LEAD. (TERNE PLATE.)

A terne plate standing seam roof

Roll Roofing has been around for a long time. This optimistic view is taken from a 19th-century advertisement.

Wooden shingles were by far the cheapest and commonest roof covering in this country until the beginning of the 20th century. The composition or asphalt shingle made its appearance at this time and quickly became established as the most popular roof covering of the new century. Asphalt shingles are today unquestionably the cheapest and quickest way to keep the rain out of your old-house, but unfortunately are *not* the most attractive or authentic solution.

Today's cedar shingles are roughly five times as expensive as their asphalt imitators, yet I unhesitatingly recommend them for old-house work. There are few building materials more rewarding to work with than these fragrant shingles, both in terms of pleasurable application and quality of the finished product. Well-laid cedar shingles make a highly attractive, long-lasting (forty years), authentic, and almost "living" roof (it's actually capable of growing tighter the harder it rains, due to the cross-grain expansion of the shingles as they absorb water).

When making the often difficult decision between a cedar or asphalt roof, you must bear in mind that cedar lasts approximately *two times* longer than asphalt, thus considerably lessening the economic gap between the two. This is moreover undoubtedly one of those places where we should strongly resist the temptation

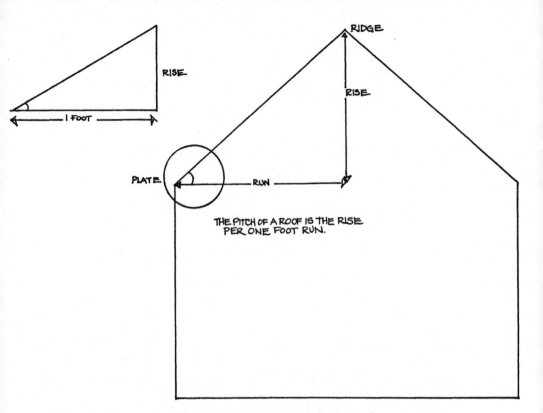

How to determine the pitch of a roof

of putting financial considerations ahead of aesthetic ones, for the roof of an old-house is very often one of its most prominent architectural features.

Regardless of financial or aesthetic considerations, cedar shingles should never be applied to roofs with a pitch of less than 3″ vertical rise per foot of horizontal run or they will be vulnerable to leakage in certain situations. Most old-houses fortunately have far steeper pitches than this minimum, permitting you to lay shingles with slightly less than one-third of their length exposed to the weather. This exposure will ensure that every point in the roof is covered by three thicknesses of shingles, a requisite of a tight cedar roof.

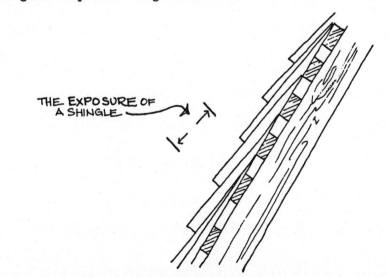

2 NAILS SECURING EACH SHINGLE ABOUT 1" FROM THEIR EDGES AND 2" ABOVE THEIR LINE OF EXPOSURE.

1½" MINIMUM OF 1½" BETWEEN JOINTS.

MAXIMUM EXPOSURE OF 5½" FOR AN 18" SHINGLE.

5½"

SHINGLES LAID ON 1 x 3 SHINGLE LATH.

1" OVERHANG OVER FASCIA HERE

2" OVERHANG OVER FASCIA HERE.

JOINTS IN ALTERNATE COURSES SHOULDN'T BE IN LINE.

Well-laid cedar shingles should have . . .

Cedar shingles (unlike their asphalt counterparts) should never be laid over one or more layers of old roofing, which should be stripped down to the roof boards, or roofers, before they are applied. The roofers may be wide and irregular, with gaping cracks between them, but such voids actually facilitate ventilation of the underside of the shingles. The ideal surface to which to apply shingles is indeed one in which boards of 2" or 3" width (known as shingle lath) alternate with spaces of approximately equal width. A cedar roof laid on such a surface will be able to breathe freely and will consequently last considerably longer than one applied to a solid roof deck.

Both white and red cedar shingles are presently available, with white being considerably less expensive and somewhat lower quality than the red. Each of them comes packed in bundles, four of which will cover one square of roof surface. They come in four different grades, with a wide price variation from lowest to highest. I strongly recommend that you purchase the top grade shingle

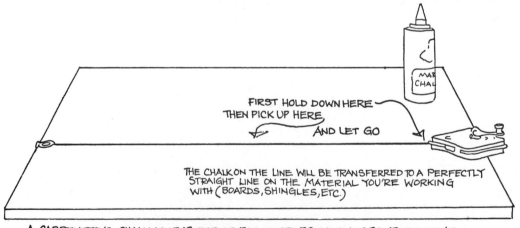

FIRST HOLD DOWN HERE
THEN PICK UP HERE,
AND LET GO

MARKING CHALK

THE CHALK ON THE LINE WILL BE TRANSFERRED TO A PERFECTLY STRAIGHT LINE ON THE MATERIAL YOU'RE WORKING WITH (BOARDS, SHINGLES, ETC.)

A CARPENTER'S CHALK LINE IS ONE OF THE SIMPLEST AND LEAST EXPENSIVE, YET INGENIOUS AND USEFUL TOOLS EVER INVENTED.

How to snap a chalk line

for use on roofs, as anything less will be false economy. The top-of-the-line red cedar shingle is known as a "number one perfection," while the best white cedar is called "extra clear."

Each shingle must be nailed with two galvanized shingle nails, placed about 2" above its line of exposure and 1" from its edges. These nails shouldn't be driven all the way home, for this crushes the wood surrounding them, providing a place for water to collect and consequent inroads of fungi in the years to come. It's also of extreme importance to leave a space of about 5⁄16" between each shingle and its neighbors, in order to allow them to expand freely when they become water-soaked. Failure to observe this may result in severe buckling and failure of the roof.

The bottom course of shingles on a roof must be laid double and should overhang the eaves by about 2". You must take care as you lay succeeding courses to allow a minimum offset of 1½" between joints in both adjacent and alternate courses. This practice will provide insurance against the possibility that an intervening shingle may someday split in such a way that three joints will be in line, thus causing a leak. As all shingles are prone to splitting in time, neglecting to take this precaution will result in a shorter-lived roof. You should also split in two every shingle wider than 8" or 10" before laying it, as only then can you be sure of where that inevitable crack will fall.

In order to keep the exposure of the shingles uniform, you should lay them to a chalk line snapped on the previous course (in order to save time, two such lines may be snapped at once and two courses laid simultaneously—the upper line will be visible through the spaces left between shingles). You may let the shingles hang over the edges of the roof in an irregular line for the present, just making

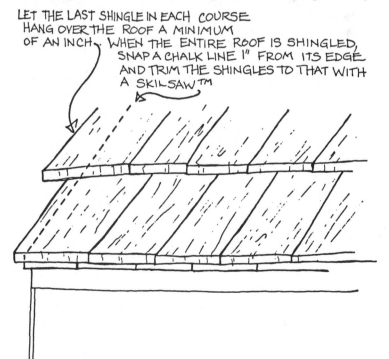

LET THE LAST SHINGLE IN EACH COURSE HANG OVER THE ROOF A MINIMUM OF AN INCH. WHEN THE ENTIRE ROOF IS SHINGLED, SNAP A CHALK LINE 1" FROM ITS EDGE AND TRIM THE SHINGLES TO THAT WITH A SKILSAW™

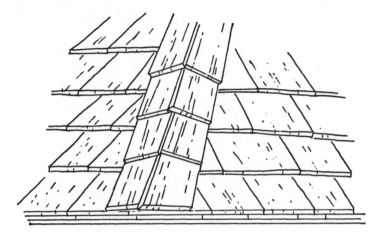

A SHINGLED HIPCAP OR RIDGE IS A BIT OF WORK,
BUT ITS APPEARANCE IS WELL WORTH THE EFFORT.

sure they project at least 1″ beyond. When you've completed the whole side of the roof, strike a chalk line parallel with the edge of the roof and ¾″ out from it and cut the ragged edge to this line with a Skilsaw.

When you must lay cedar shingles to a valley, or trough formed by the intersection of two roofs, strike a chalk line 3″ or 4″ on either side of its center, making sure they are slightly further apart at its bottom than at its top. This will keep ice from wedging in it during the winter. Next cut a very wide shingle to the angle formed by one of these chalk lines and the line of a course of shingles that will abut the valley. You may now use this shingle as a pattern for several dozen others with which you may start subsequent courses as you work your way up the valley.

Although ridges and hips (sloping ridges formed by the intersection of two roofs) are the least vulnerable parts of a roof (water always runs away from them), they are among the most prominent visually. A strip of sheet metal or a pair of boards would more than suffice to protect them from the weather, but might do much to detract from an otherwise beautiful roof. The far greater labor involved in shingling hips and ridges is thus more than justified by their far more pleasing appearance.

All this presupposes that you are laying an entire new roof, but how can you replace a few bad shingles in an otherwise sound covering? This seemingly impossible feat may easily be performed with the aid of a special tool called a shingle-thief. Slide it under one of the shingles to be removed and sweep it down and across until one of its hooks engages one of the two nails that secure the shingle. Now strike the flattened portion of the tool with a hammer or shingling hatchet until the nail pulls free. Repeat this process with the other nail and the shingle may easily be removed and a new one inserted in its place.

In order to secure this new shingle without resorting to exposed nails (which are inevitably the cause of leaks on roofs), I use a trick taught me by the old Nantucket craftsman. First push the new shingle into place until only an inch of it is left projecting below the butts of its neighbors. Now drive the usual two shingle nails at approximately 45° angles into the joint between the new shingle and the

REMOVING A SHINGLE FROM A ROOF OR WALL

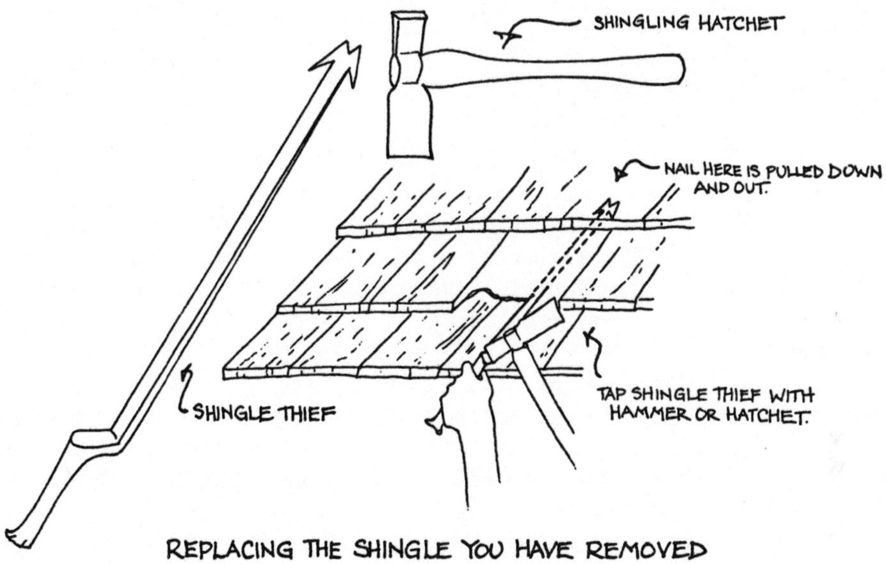

SHINGLING HATCHET

NAIL HERE IS PULLED DOWN AND OUT.

SHINGLE THIEF

TAP SHINGLE THIEF WITH HAMMER OR HATCHET.

REPLACING THE SHINGLE YOU HAVE REMOVED

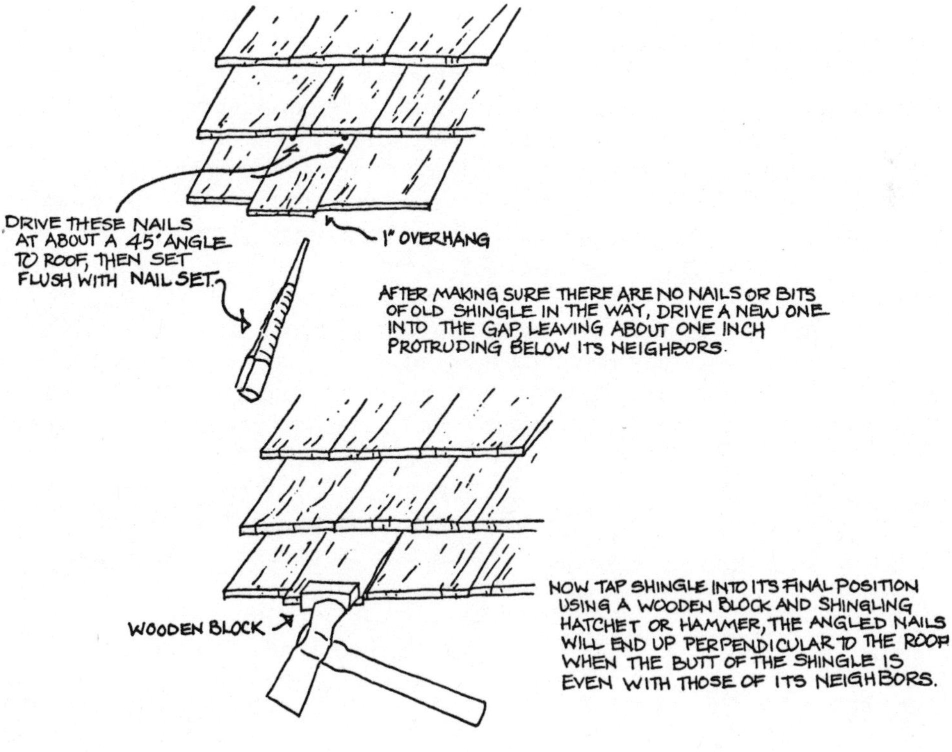

DRIVE THESE NAILS AT ABOUT A 45° ANGLE TO ROOF, THEN SET FLUSH WITH NAIL SET.

1" OVERHANG

AFTER MAKING SURE THERE ARE NO NAILS OR BITS OF OLD SHINGLE IN THE WAY, DRIVE A NEW ONE INTO THE GAP, LEAVING ABOUT ONE INCH PROTRUDING BELOW ITS NEIGHBORS.

WOODEN BLOCK

NOW TAP SHINGLE INTO ITS FINAL POSITION USING A WOODEN BLOCK AND SHINGLING HATCHET OR HAMMER, THE ANGLED NAILS WILL END UP PERPENDICULAR TO THE ROOF WHEN THE BUTT OF THE SHINGLE IS EVEN WITH THOSE OF ITS NEIGHBORS.

butt of the one above it. Set these nails slightly below the surface with a nailset (contradicting my previous admonition to the contrary in this particular instance) and drive the shingle all the way home with a wood block and hammer. The nails that secure the shingle will then be straight up and down and completely out of sight, 1″ above the line of exposure.

The most vulnerable points in any roof are its valleys and its intersections with vents, chimneys, skylights, and dormer windows. These critical areas must be meticulously covered with sheet metal flashing to prevent leakage. The tendency today is to use very thin, bright aluminum flashing, but I find it wholly inappropriate to cedar shingles and to an old-house, both on practical and aesthetic grounds. There are three flashing materials that *are* compatible with a cedar roof on an old-house, in terms of beauty, workability, and longevity: lead, copper, and terne.

In New England, where the old traditions are still strong, lead is still the standard for chimney flashing, even on new homes. It's a wonderfully durable material, even when exposed to strong salt air (which destroys aluminum in a short time). It also has the unique capability of being so malleable that it may be beaten around the corner of a chimney into a jointless three-dimensional corner.

Copper is the king of flashing materials, being extremely long-lasting, a delight to work with and a beauty to behold. It isn't as malleable as lead, but may be easily bent into any position *except* a three-dimensional corner and is extremely easy to solder. The only shortcomings of copper and lead as flashing materials are their softness and costliness.

Terne plate is on the other hand relatively inexpensive (not much costlier than aluminum), not too soft, easily bent and soldered, relatively long-lasting, and not unattractive to the eye or hand. I have found that 20 or 40 pound terne is an excellent alternative to the more costly lead or copper flashing on a high-quality old-house roof. Examine the flashing that now protects the vulnerable areas of your roof: if it's copper or lead, it almost certainly may be reused, but if it's aluminum or rotted terne or galvanized iron, replace it with copper, lead, or new terne.

Although they are the most vulnerable parts of a roof, you may easily flash valleys with a continuous length of flashing (no less than 20″ wide), laying half of it on each of the roofs forming the valley. Plumbing vent pipes that protrude through the roof are also easily flashed with special roof flanges available from building or plumbing supply dealers. Try to get DWV (drain-waste-vent) flanges made of copper with a lead ring that may be beaten tightly against the vent pipe, for they will be far more compatible with a cedar roof than the more popular neoprene substitutes.

Wherever the slope of a roof butts against a wall, as where it meets the ver-

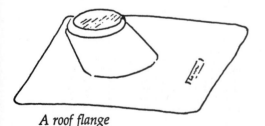

A roof flange

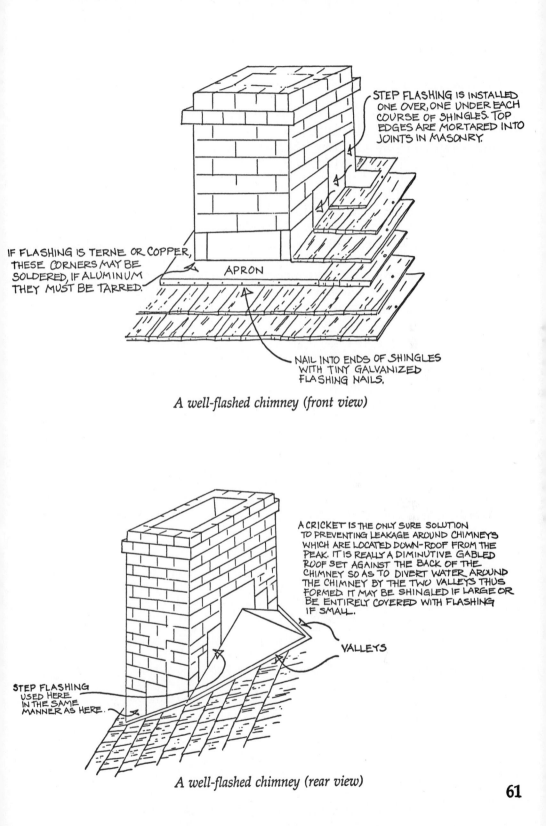

STEP FLASHING IS INSTALLED ONE OVER, ONE UNDER EACH COURSE OF SHINGLES. TOP EDGES ARE MORTARED INTO JOINTS IN MASONRY.

IF FLASHING IS TERNE OR COPPER, THESE CORNERS MAY BE SOLDERED, IF ALUMINUM THEY MUST BE TARRED.

APRON

NAIL INTO ENDS OF SHINGLES WITH TINY GALVANIZED FLASHING NAILS.

A well-flashed chimney (front view)

A CRICKET IS THE ONLY SURE SOLUTION TO PREVENTING LEAKAGE AROUND CHIMNEYS WHICH ARE LOCATED DOWN-ROOF FROM THE PEAK. IT IS REALLY A DIMINUTIVE GABLED ROOF SET AGAINST THE BACK OF THE CHIMNEY SO AS TO DIVERT WATER AROUND THE CHIMNEY BY THE TWO VALLEYS THUS FORMED IT MAY BE SHINGLED IF LARGE OR BE ENTIRELY COVERED WITH FLASHING IF SMALL.

VALLEYS

STEP FLASHING USED HERE IN THE SAME MANNER AS HERE.

A well-flashed chimney (rear view)

61

tical side of a dormer (a small, windowed gable projecting from a roof), their line of intersection must be stepflashed with 8″ squares of flashing. Each of these should be bent in the middle so that half lies on the roof and half on the dormer wall (under the siding) and laid between successive courses of shingles in such a manner that they are just covered by them. The flashing will then overlap itself by 2″ to 3″ (depending on the exposure of the shingles) and will ensure a leakproof roof.

The most difficult part of a roof to flash is its intersection with a chimney (or skylight, but you're not as likely to encounter these on old-house roofs). The front or down-roof surface of a chimney (as well as the front of a dormer which begins up-roof from the house wall) must be flashed with a sheet metal apron that covers its lower 4″ (or more) and the last course of shingles below it. The apron must also project several inches up the roof along and on the sides of the chimney, thus allowing stepflashing to generously overlap it. The points formed by the intersection of the chimney's front corners and the roof are extremely vulnerable to leakage. These points (as well as the entire corner) may be neatly soldered if you are using copper or terne flashing, but they must be tarred if aluminum is used.

The apron and chimney stepflashing may merely be bent over and mortared into grooves raked out of the joints between the chimney's bricks or stones or it may be cut off slightly below these joints. In this case it is known as base flashing and must be overlapped with cap flashing, which is mortared into the chimney as before. This two-piece system is known as flashing and counterflashing and has the distinct advantage of permitting unequal movement of chimney and roof without consequent tearing or dislodging of the flashing.

The most vulnerable side of a chimney is nevertheless that facing up-roof, particularly if it's at a considerable distance from the ridge (chimneys that actually intersect the ridge don't share this vulnerability). Rain or snow is inevitably trapped behind a down-roof chimney in its otherwise unobstructed descent of the

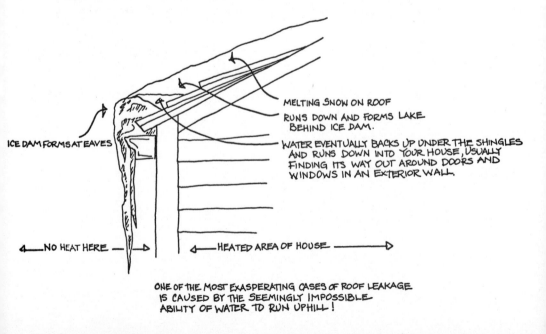

MELTING SNOW ON ROOF

RUNS DOWN AND FORMS LAKE BEHIND ICE DAM.

ICE DAM FORMS AT EAVES

WATER EVENTUALLY BACKS UP UNDER THE SHINGLES AND RUNS DOWN INTO YOUR HOUSE, USUALLY FINDING ITS WAY OUT AROUND DOORS AND WINDOWS IN AN EXTERIOR WALL.

◄──NO HEAT HERE ──▷   ◄───── HEATED AREA OF HOUSE ─────▷

ONE OF THE MOST EXASPERATING CASES OF ROOF LEAKAGE IS CAUSED BY THE SEEMINGLY IMPOSSIBLE ABILITY OF WATER TO RUN UPHILL!

roof and will find its way inside the house if there be but the tiniest flaw in flashing or roofing. Fortunately this situation may be virtually eliminated by the construction of a miniature gabled roof called a cricket behind the chimney, thereby creating two short valleys that will carry water to either side of it. These valleys are flashed like any others, with their ends overlapping the stepflashing along the chimney's sides; and the back of the chimney (which now abuts the two opposing slopes formed by the cricket) is stepflashed in the same manner as its sides.

Another part of your roof that may be unexpectedly susceptible to leaking during a hard winter is the first 2' or 3' above its eaves. When snow on the roof is

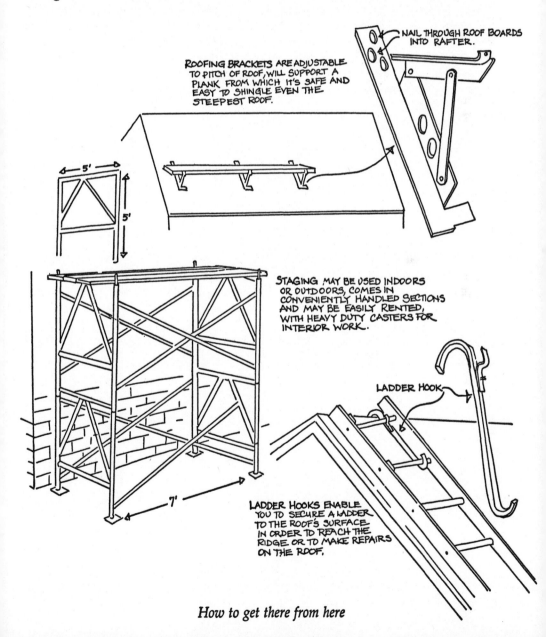

NAIL THROUGH ROOF BOARDS INTO RAFTER.

ROOFING BRACKETS ARE ADJUSTABLE TO PITCH OF ROOF, WILL SUPPORT A PLANK FROM WHICH IT'S SAFE AND EASY TO SHINGLE EVEN THE STEEPEST ROOF.

STAGING MAY BE USED INDOORS OR OUTDOORS, COMES IN CONVENIENTLY HANDLED SECTIONS AND MAY BE EASILY RENTED, WITH HEAVY DUTY CASTERS FOR INTERIOR WORK.

LADDER HOOK

LADDER HOOKS ENABLE YOU TO SECURE A LADDER TO THE ROOF'S SURFACE IN ORDER TO REACH THE RIDGE OR TO MAKE REPAIRS ON THE ROOF.

How to get there from here

melted by the heat that may escape from your house on a cold January night, the resultant water will run down the roof until it encounters the unheated portion beyond the outside wall, where it refreezes. This process gradually causes the formation of an ice dam, behind which subsequent run-off collects, eventually forming a trough of water that may back up under the shingles and into your house.

Although many people attack this problem by fastening electric heat tape along this vulnerable area, a more permanent and eventually economical solution is the installation of a continuous sheet of flashing along the bottom of your roof (making sure it projects 1' or more up the roof from the inside of the outside wall). A simpler, yet perhaps not altogether satisfactory solution to the problem was once reportedly proposed by Frank Lloyd Wright in response to a criticism of the snow-load bearing capacity of one of his northerly creations: "If you can afford me as an architect," Wright replied, "then surely you can afford to hire a small boy to shovel snow off the roof."

6

The Skin: Wall, Ceiling, and Floor Coverings

Both our bodies and our houses obviously require protective envelopes to shield them from the severity of the weather. It is therefore not surprising that the architectural term for the siding and underlying sheathing that cover an old-house's skeleton is *skin*. Somewhat less obviously, a similar protective membrane covers the inner cavities of our bodies (the linings of the mouth, nasal passages, and stomach among others) and our old-house's interior surfaces (interior wall, ceiling, and floor coverings).

The earliest type of siding used to cover the walls of colonial American homes was clapboarding. Such clapboards (pronounced "clabberds") were riven from blocks of oak with a froe and dressed to a taper with a drawknife in the same manner as shingles. These 3' to 6' boards were nailed directly to the studs so that they overlapped each other 1" or more, providing a weather-tight surface. Riven clapboards became obsolete shortly after the advent of the circular saw in 1825, after which sawn, tapered weatherboards of pine (the forerunners of today's beveled cedar siding) became the favorite skin of houses for many years.

White pine shingles were also used to cover the walls of some of the earliest houses in New England. Their use gradually increased until, by the end of the 19th century, they were available in every lumberyard in the country (although usually made of red or white cedar) in a variety of ornamental shapes, such as diamonds and scallops, as well as the usual taper-sawn rectangles.

You may lay sidewall shingles in much the same manner as those on a roof, **65**

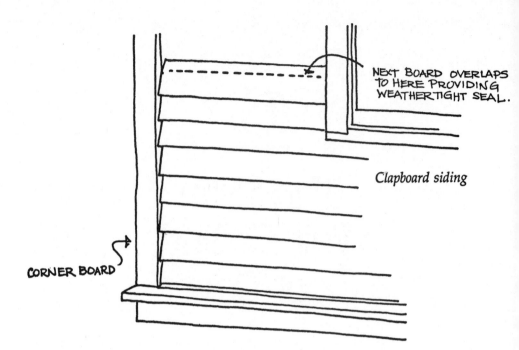

NEXT BOARD OVERLAPS TO HERE PROVIDING WEATHERTIGHT SEAL.

Clapboard siding

CORNER BOARD

with two important differences. Due to their less exposed location, it's not necessary to worry about alternate-course joints lining up nor is it necessary to leave expansion cracks between them. On the contrary, you should fit them tightly against one another, to prevent rain from driving in.

Although clapboards were nailed directly to the studs, this was obviously impossible for shingle siding. A layer of 1"-thick sheathing boards was therefore first nailed to the frame of houses to be shingled, providing greater structural strength and thermal insulation, as well as a surface to which to secure the shingles.

By the middle of the 18th century it had become standard practice to sheath all well-constructed buildings, regardless of the type of siding used. These boards were laid horizontally (sometimes vertically) until the advent of the balloon frame, when it became necessary to lay them diagonally to provide that skeleton with the additional structural strength it required. Each board thus became a partial corner

Shingle siding

SIDEWALL SHINGLES ARE LAID TIGHT AGAINST EACH OTHER, UNLIKE ROOF SHINGLES.

DOUBLE FIRST COURSE

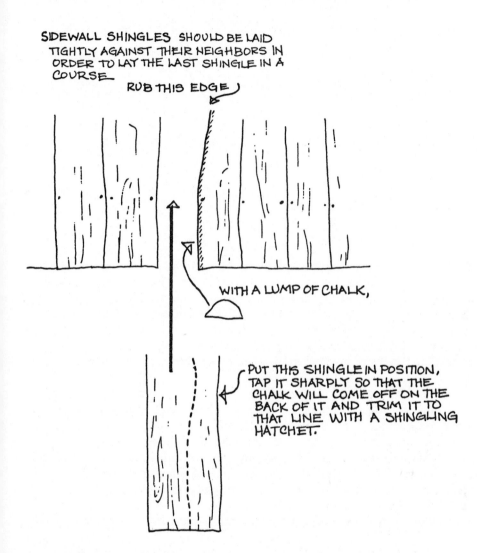

SIDEWALL SHINGLES SHOULD BE LAID TIGHTLY AGAINST THEIR NEIGHBORS IN ORDER TO LAY THE LAST SHINGLE IN A COURSE

RUB THIS EDGE

WITH A LUMP OF CHALK,

PUT THIS SHINGLE IN POSITION, TAP IT SHARPLY SO THAT THE CHALK WILL COME OFF ON THE BACK OF IT AND TRIM IT TO THAT LINE WITH A SHINGLING HATCHET.

brace, replacing in aggregate those single members so effective in the braced frame. Sheathing boards were wide, square-edged, and rough-sawn until the early 1900s, when they were succeeded by narrower, machine-planed shiplap or tongue-and-groove sheathing.

Some early old-houses were also sided with hand-planed, square-edged, and unbeveled pine boards laid like clapboards, known as colonial siding. During the Gothic Revival in the early 19th century, similar boards were laid vertically with narrow strips of wood covering the joints between them, comprising the attractive and economical board and batten siding, which has recently returned to favor. Novelty siding (consisting of horizontally laid shiplap decorated with molded concavities) made its appearance during the early 1900s and still has a limited use today.

Many otherwise dignified old-houses have unfortunately been made to appear ridiculous by the ill-advised replacement of their original siding with new and inappropriate styles. Don't despair if the beauty of your house has been

67

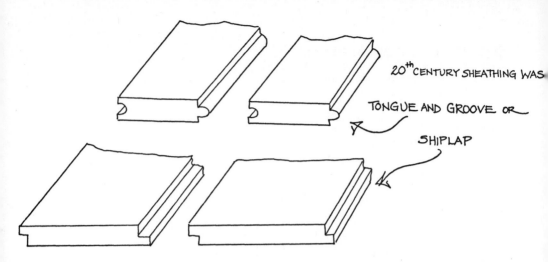

disfigured by asbestos shingles, asphalt-brick paper, or vinyl or aluminum siding, however, for it's quite likely its installers never bothered to remove the underlying siding. (The U.S. Secretary of the Interior's Standards for Historic Preservation Projects strongly recommends against the use of any such material.) I once brought about a most spectacular transformation of an old-house by simply removing the layer of institutional green asbestos shingles covering its original clapboarding (badly in need of painting but otherwise in a perfect state of preservation).

Some old-houses had interior skins that closely resembled their exteriors, such as those formed of horizontal wide pine sheathing boards or vertical board and batten paneling (the forerunner of the later siding). The fireplace and stair walls of more elegant dwellings were often treated to the attentions of a master cabinetmaker, who displayed his virtuosity in a symphony of hand-planed moldings and panels. (See description of panel door in the next chapter). This was true paneling, unlike the thin plywood sham that has unconscionably borrowed the good name of its predecessor.

The first usurper of this name was actually the late-19th-century paneling

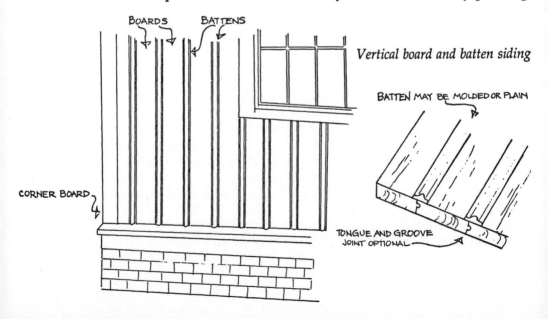

BOARDS   BATTENS

Vertical board and batten siding

BATTEN MAY BE MOLDED OR PLAIN

CORNER BOARD

TONGUE AND GROOVE
JOINT OPTIONAL

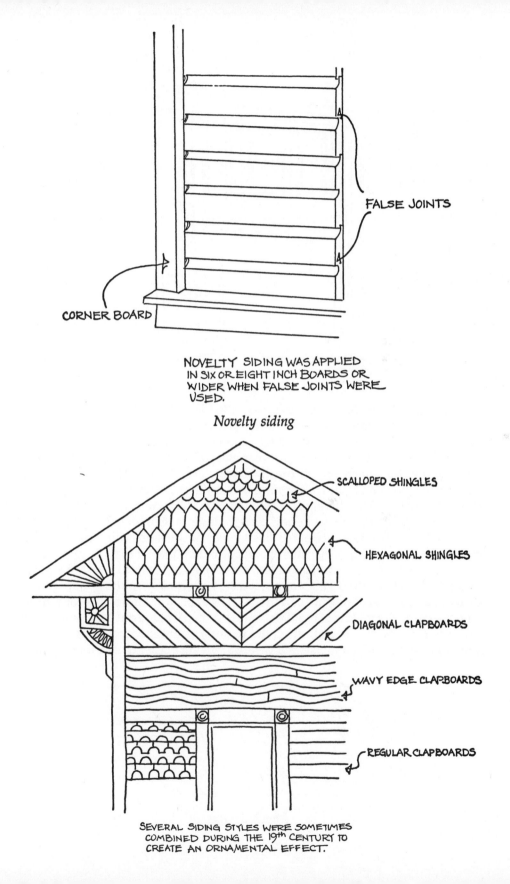

FALSE JOINTS

CORNER BOARD

NOVELTY SIDING WAS APPLIED
IN SIX OR EIGHT INCH BOARDS OR
WIDER WHEN FALSE JOINTS WERE
USED.

Novelty siding

SCALLOPED SHINGLES

HEXAGONAL SHINGLES

DIAGONAL CLAPBOARDS

WAVY EDGE CLAPBOARDS

REGULAR CLAPBOARDS

SEVERAL SIDING STYLES WERE SOMETIMES
COMBINED DURING THE 19th CENTURY TO
CREATE AN ORNAMENTAL EFFECT.

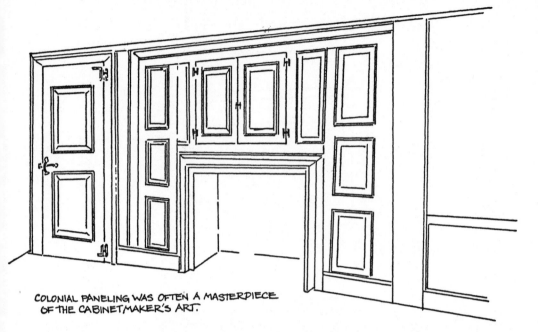

COLONIAL PANELING WAS OFTEN A MASTERPIECE
OF THE CABINETMAKER'S ART.

known as matchboarding, composed of beaded ⅜" to ¾" thick tongue-and-groove boards of 3" to 4" width. Although entire walls were sometimes covered with these boards, their use was usually restricted to ceilings or the first 3' or 4' of wall surfaces. This last extremely popular use of matchboarding is known as wainscoting, for which reason the two terms are often incorrectly used interchangeably (you can't put wainscoting on a ceiling). Matchboarding has made a recent return to the lumberyard, where I hope it will compete favorably with the 4' × 8' sheets of "Provincial Pecan" and "Mediterranean Mahogany" paneling.

The vast preponderance of old-house interior wall and ceiling surfaces were nonetheless plastered, rather than paneled. Before plaster may be applied to a wall or ceiling, a suitable surface of lath must be nailed to it, to which the plaster may adhere. The earliest lath was obtained by alternately splitting a board from each of its ends and pulling it apart in the manner of an accordion. Accordion lath was used until the middle of the 19th century, when it faded out of popularity due to the availability of sawn lath from the recently established sawmills. All wood lath must be thoroughly moistened before applying plaster to it or it will pull the

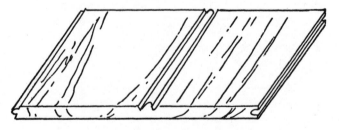

water out of the plaster, causing plaster dry-out and resultant weakness and cracking.

Expanded-rib metal lath was developed during the very end of the 19th century, greatly surpassing its predecessors in strength and ease of installation. It's still manufactured in 27" by 8' sheets of various configurations. Rocklath, a cousin of the popular gypsum wallboard Sheetrock, was put on the market early in the century and is still available in 16" by 4' sheets today, although not all building supply dealers are aware of this.

No matter which type of lath you use, its primary function is to provide a surface to which plaster may tightly adhere. Although this is accomplished to some degree by surface adhesion (particularly in the case of Rocklath), the strength of plaster is usually determined by the quality of its keying. This occurs when some of the wet plaster is pushed through the spaces in or between the lath and spreads out behind it, forming (when hardened) a strong mechanical key.

Plaster lath

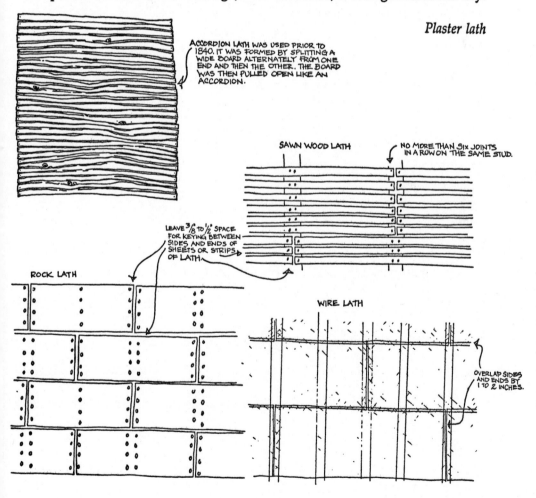

ACCORDION LATH WAS USED PRIOR TO 1840. IT WAS FORMED BY SPLITTING A WIDE BOARD ALTERNATELY FROM ONE END AND THEN THE OTHER. THE BOARD WAS THEN PULLED OPEN LIKE AN ACCORDION.

SAWN WOOD LATH

NO MORE THAN SIX JOINTS IN A ROW ON THE SAME STUD.

LEAVE 3/8 TO 1/2" SPACE FOR KEYING BETWEEN SIDES AND ENDS OF SHEETS OR STRIPS OF LATH.

ROCK LATH

WIRE LATH

OVERLAP SIDES AND ENDS BY 1 TO 2 INCHES.

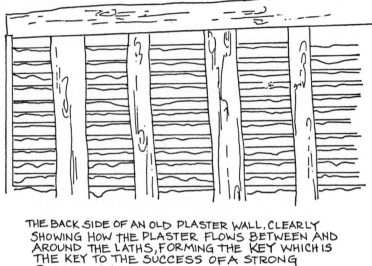

THE BACK SIDE OF AN OLD PLASTER WALL, CLEARLY
SHOWING HOW THE PLASTER FLOWS BETWEEN AND
AROUND THE LATHS, FORMING THE KEY WHICH IS
THE KEY TO THE SUCCESS OF A STRONG
PLASTER WALL.

Plaster keying

Since metal lath is filled with holes through which plaster may ooze, it provides the best opportunity for keying to occur. Wood lath is next best in this regard and Rocklath the poorest, as keying can only occur at the edges of each sheet.

The methods of plastering have changed very little from early colonial times right up until the 20th century. A top quality plaster job was applied in three successive coats. The first, or scratch, coat, rich in lime (sometimes in the form of pulverized seashells) and cow hair (for strength), was applied directly to the wet

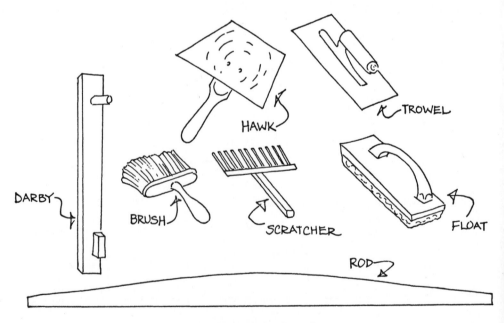

DARBY

HAWK

TROWEL

BRUSH

SCRATCHER

FLOAT

ROD

A plasterer's basic tools

wood lath with a plasterer's trowel. After this first coat was completed but as yet unhardened, it was crosshatched with a sharp stick or metal scratcher to facilitate the bonding of the second, or brown coat. Rich in sand and cow hair, this coat would be applied after the first had dried, with a nearly 4'-long trowel known as a darby and trued with an even longer straightedge called a rod to ensure a straight and flat surface.

After the brown coat had in turn dried, a thin coat of plaster rich in lime but containing no hair was troweled over it to obtain a smooth, hard, and durable surface. This result was facilitated by sprinkling it with water during the course of its application. The same basic procedure for a first quality plaster job should still be followed today, although the composition of plaster has changed considerably over the years. Modern plasters have bases of gypsum rather than lime, use fiber glass instead of cow hair for strength (only required over wood lath), and include a lightweight aggregate, such as vermiculite or perlite, which greatly reduce the plaster's weight. It sometimes isn't easy to find plaster today (as it can't be stored for too long without picking up water from the air and becoming unusable), but at least one building supply dealer in your locality should stock it, perhaps under the trade name, Gypsolite or Structolite.

If your old-house has plaster walls and ceilings that appear to be in the last stages of disrepair, don't jump to the conclusion that they must be demolished or covered with Sheetrock, for it's often possible to effectively patch old plaster that might at first seem unredeemable. You should make every effort to save as many of the original interior surfaces of your house as possible, for they contribute greatly to its feeling and authenticity.

You may easily fill cracks and very small holes in plaster with Sheetrock joint compound (very inexpensively available in handy, reusable five-gallon pails), used in combination with a special fiber glass tape to prevent recracking. This cracks badly when used to fill large, deep holes and thus is unsuitable for this purpose. The extremely fast-setting plaster of Paris may be used to fill slightly larger holes and patching plaster for still larger ones. If areas of plaster are intact, yet bulge ominously (a very common plight of ceilings), the plaster's keys have broken off behind its lath. You may often remedy this situation by securing such areas to the studs or joists with countersunk washers and screws or roofing disks and nails.

If you have truly unsalvageable plaster or are adding entirely new walls or ceilings to your old-house, should you cover them with plaster or Sheetrock? Faced with the prospect of a laborious three-coat plaster job compared with the ease of slapping up 4' × 8' sheets of Sheetrock, most people don't give plaster more than a moment's consideration. This attitude is unfortunate (although completely understandable), for few things are as out of place in an old-house as Sheetrock, unless it be aluminum siding or plywood paneling.

Rocklath fortunately provides a good compromise in such situations. It's as inexpensive as Sheetrock, is easier if not quicker to install (as it comes in smaller sheets) and most importantly, you may obtain a strong and attractive job by applying only one coat of plaster over it. If you think that's still one more coat than

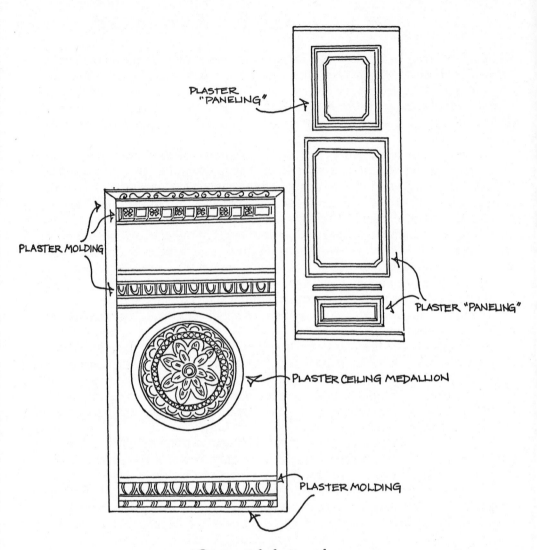

PLASTER "PANELING"

PLASTER MOLDING

PLASTER "PANELING"

PLASTER CEILING MEDALLION

PLASTER MOLDING

Ornamental plasterwork

you would need over Sheetrock, consider that *three* coats of joint compound are necessary to hide Sheetrock joints and nail holes. Applying Rocklath and one coat of roughish plaster over it requires no greater expenditure of time and money than Sheetrocking and taping and if anything takes less skill to execute. I'm nevertheless not recommending it as a substitute for a three-coat job (if you're inclined to go that route, go right ahead—you'll get the best), but only to dissuade you from using Sheetrock.

The earliest floors were formed of single layers of hand-planed wide pine boards, joined together with splines, which are thin strips of wood fitted into grooves in the edges of the floorboards. The grain of these splines usually ran at right angles to the flooring, rendering a splined joint less likely to split than that between two tongue-and-groove boards. Early floorboards were often tapered,

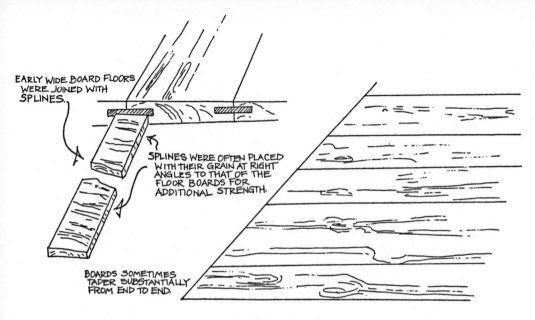

EARLY WIDE BOARD FLOORS WERE JOINED WITH SPLINES.

SPLINES WERE OFTEN PLACED WITH THEIR GRAIN AT RIGHT ANGLES TO THAT OF THE FLOOR BOARDS FOR ADDITIONAL STRENGTH.

BOARDS SOMETIMES TAPER SUBSTANTIALLY FROM END TO END.

Wide pine floors

representing the maximum that could be cut from a tapered log. If you ever have to take up a floor of this kind, be sure for this reason to mark the position of each board or you might have considerable trouble in relaying it.

Antique wide pine floorboards are very difficult to find today and usually bring a premium price when they are available. Close approximations may nevertheless still be obtained from the few scattered sawmills having access to large-diameter Eastern white pine logs. I recently had the good fortune to purchase a fine stack of 14″ to 20″ wide pine boards from such a small mill in the Catskill Mountains of New York state, and I've heard of New England mills that will cut boards up to 3′ wide.

As handsome as pine floors are, they are very soft and consequently show signs of wear quickly (this *can* be considered part of an old-house's charm, but isn't appreciated by everyone). It must certainly have been a large factor in the

ROUGH SAWN BOARDS USED TO BE SMOOTHED WITH A WOODEN TRY PLANE.

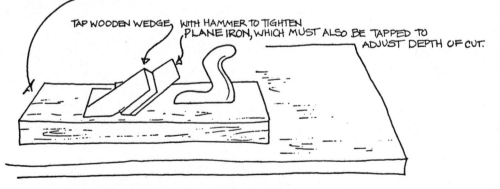

TAP WOODEN WEDGE WITH HAMMER TO TIGHTEN PLANE IRON, WHICH MUST ALSO BE TAPPED TO ADJUST DEPTH OF CUT.

THE TEXTURE OF AN OLD BOARD SMOOTHED WITH THIS PLANE IS SUBTLE, YET UNMISTAKABLE. IF YOU SHINE A LIGHT AT A LOW ANGLE ACROSS IT, THE SLIGHT CONCAVITIES FORMED BY THIS OLD PLANE BECOME READILY APPARENT.

quick rise to popularity during the last half of the 19th century of the far more durable oak, maple, and cherry tongue-and-groove flooring.

The crowning glory of hardwood floors laid during that time was the parquet floor, in which myriads of tiny pieces of wood of differing species are arranged in sometimes intricate patterns. These floors appear to be the creations of the most gifted craftsmen, but in truth aren't quite so deserving of praise, as parquet was purchased in precut squares on a cloth or paper backing, which were then glued to the subfloor. You may have the chance (as I did once) to become such a craftsman yourself, however, if parts of your parquet floor are missing, for you won't be able to obtain replacement squares for it—you'll have to make your own.

The thickness of a parquet floor might have originally been as much as ⅜" or as little as ¼" and can grow much thinner after many years of use, particularly in

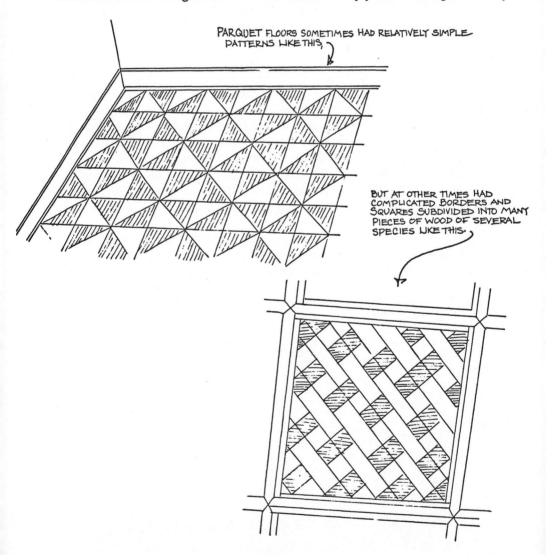

PARQUET FLOORS SOMETIMES HAD RELATIVELY SIMPLE PATTERNS LIKE THIS,

BUT AT OTHER TIMES HAD COMPLICATED BORDERS AND SQUARES SUBDIVIDED INTO MANY PIECES OF WOOD OF SEVERAL SPECIES LIKE THIS.

Parquet floors

areas with the most traffic, such as halls and doorways. You should consequently be very careful sanding parquet floors, for it's all too easy to sand the last sixteenth of an inch of wood away in front of a doorway and be left with nothing but the subfloor beneath.

During the early 1900s many people developed a passion for covering the floors of their houses with linoleum. They often wouldn't even bother to remove it when it had worn out, but would merely cover it with a new layer, allowing the thicknesses to accumulate over the years like wallpaper. Linoleum is fortunately easily removed in most cases, for it was usually only tacked to the floor. Once you've removed it, you may add it to the pile of asbestos shingles and plywood paneling you may already have made.

7

Doors and Windows: The Organs of the Senses

No other portion of the anatomy of an old-house contributes more to its external appearance and to the quality of life within than do its doors and windows. The counterparts of our eyes, nose, and ears, they are the openings in the structure's skin that permit the passage of light, air, and sound (as well as allowing us to enter and leave our homes). Poor proportion or placement of doors and windows results in a host of practical and aesthetic problems, which an old-house may reflect in its sorrowful, ill-natured, or demented expression.

The earliest American doors were constructed of vertical boards reinforced by pairs of chamfered, or beveled, cleats or battens. These were fastened with wrought nails driven through both batten and board and clinched, or bent over, on the front of the door. Batten doors have been used for closet, cabinet, cellar, and attic closures until quite recently, although their battens have been secured with screws instead of wrought nails since the middle of the 19th century.

The chief disadvantage of this type of door is its vulnerability to expansion and contraction, making it unlikely that it will fit properly in its frame during both the high humidity of the summer and the extreme dryness of a winter-heated house. This inherent weakness is caused by the propensity of all wood to shrink and expand *across* its grain with such seasonal changes in temperature and humidity (this effect is negligible *along* its grain). Even though constructed of thoroughly seasoned wood, an unpainted batten door might actually gain a full ½" in width between January and August.

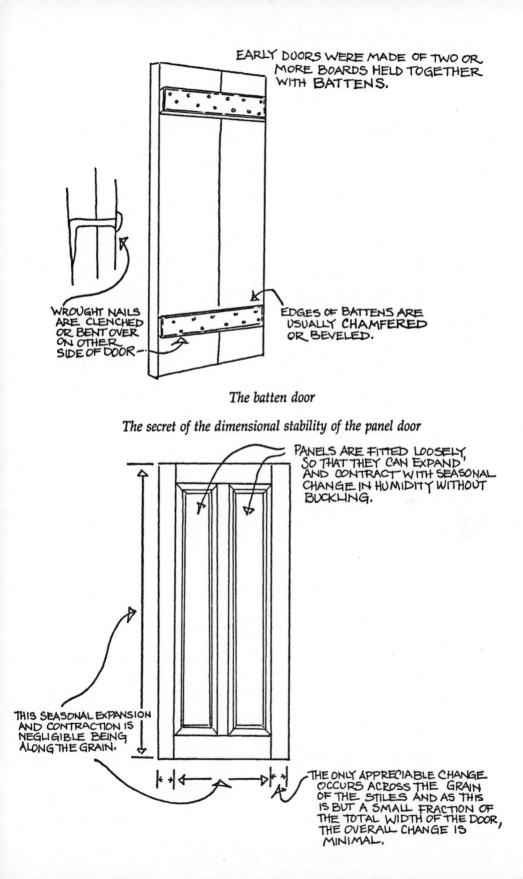

EARLY DOORS WERE MADE OF TWO OR MORE BOARDS HELD TOGETHER WITH BATTENS.

WROUGHT NAILS ARE CLENCHED OR BENT OVER ON OTHER SIDE OF DOOR.

EDGES OF BATTENS ARE USUALLY CHAMFERED OR BEVELED.

The batten door

The secret of the dimensional stability of the panel door

PANELS ARE FITTED LOOSELY, SO THAT THEY CAN EXPAND AND CONTRACT WITH SEASONAL CHANGE IN HUMIDITY WITHOUT BUCKLING.

THIS SEASONAL EXPANSION AND CONTRACTION IS NEGLIGIBLE BEING ALONG THE GRAIN.

THE ONLY APPRECIABLE CHANGE OCCURS ACROSS THE GRAIN OF THE STILES AND AS THIS IS BUT A SMALL FRACTION OF THE TOTAL WIDTH OF THE DOOR, THE OVERALL CHANGE IS MINIMAL.

The panel door first made its appearance in this country about 1700, over-coming this serious shortcoming of the batten door by the nature of its construction. It ingeniously enclosed several wooden panels in a mortised and tenoned frame, which itself retained nearly constant dimensions despite the season of the year. As the panels could expand and contract in this frame without affecting the dimensions of the door itself, its dimensional instability was limited to the cross-grain expansion of its stiles.

The construction of the panel door underwent a number of changes over the years, which could be of assistance in dating your old-house. The earliest doors had raised panels, which protruded slightly beyond their frames and were set into grooves in their stiles and rails, whose edges were molded to a quarter round. This molding was exclusively used until 1775, when its use was discontinued in favor of a bead or ogee (S-shaped) curve. Panels in doors constructed since 1835 are

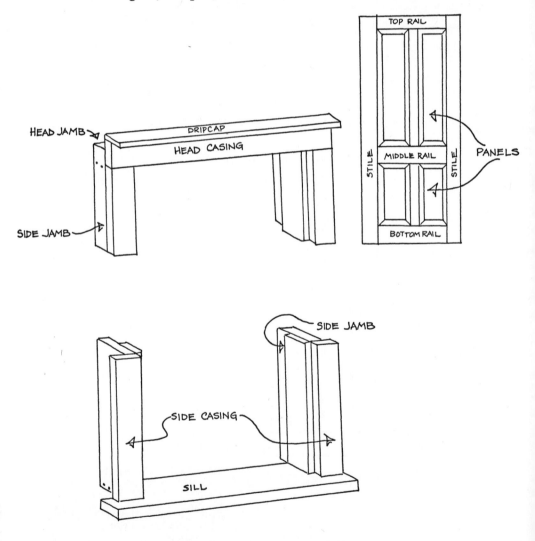

The anatomy of the panel door and its frame

slightly recessed or flush with their frames and are secured with strips of molding nailed to stiles and rails.

If you have doors in your old-house that don't open and close properly, first check their frames for squareness and plumbness. If these aren't in truth, the problem may not be with the doors themselves, but with the frame of your house. If the door frames are true, next check to make sure the butts, or hinges upon which the doors are hung, are securely fastened. Tighten the screws that secure them if they are loose or replace them with longer screws of the same diameter if they can't be tightened.

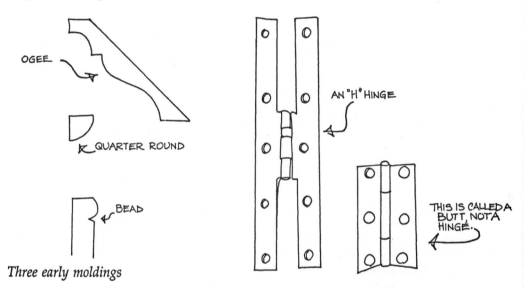

OGEE

QUARTER ROUND

BEAD

AN "H" HINGE

THIS IS CALLED A BUTT, NOT A HINGE.

Three early moldings

If you have a panel door that still won't close properly, make certain its stiles are joined tightly to its rails. If they have become separated, force glue into the gap between them and pull the door tightly together with a cabinetmaker's pipe clamp. The mortised and tenoned joints between stiles and rails may now be further secured by driving steel dowels through them. If the bottom of the door is in extremely poor condition, you can attractively reinforce it with a solid brass plate screwed to both stiles and bottom rail.

If your door still binds in its frame, rub chalk or crayon on the edge of its jambs and close it hard: The chalk will be transferred to the edge of the door wherever it's binding. You may now plane those chalk marks off until the proper clearance between door and jamb is established (you should just be able to insert a nickel between them). If you have to plane the lower part of the door down, you will have to knock the pins out of its butts with a hammer and screwdriver (or carefully remove the nails from its hinges) and remove the door from its opening.

The earliest American window sash (the usually movable portion of a window, which actually contains the glass) utilized small, diamond-shaped quarrels

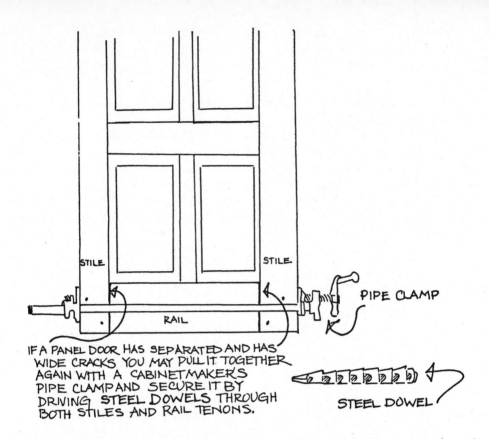

STILE

STILE

PIPE CLAMP

RAIL

IF A PANEL DOOR HAS SEPARATED AND HAS
WIDE CRACKS YOU MAY PULL IT TOGETHER
AGAIN WITH A CABINETMAKER'S
PIPE CLAMP AND SECURE IT BY
DRIVING STEEL DOWELS THROUGH
BOTH STILES AND RAIL TENONS.

STEEL DOWEL

of glass, held in place by lead calms (pronounced "cames"). These were the only sash available until 1700 and were invariably hung as outward-opening casements (sash that open and close like doors). Casement windows with many different styles of sash have been used from that time until the present. If you have any in your old-house that give you trouble, follow the same procedure as you would for doors.

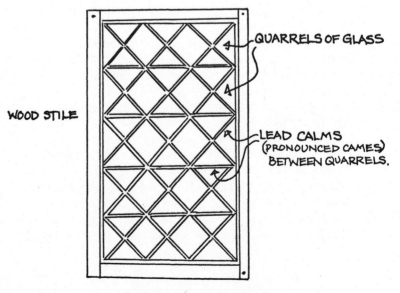

QUARRELS OF GLASS

WOOD STILE

LEAD CALMS
(PRONOUNCED CAMES)
BETWEEN QUARRELS.

17th-century casement sash

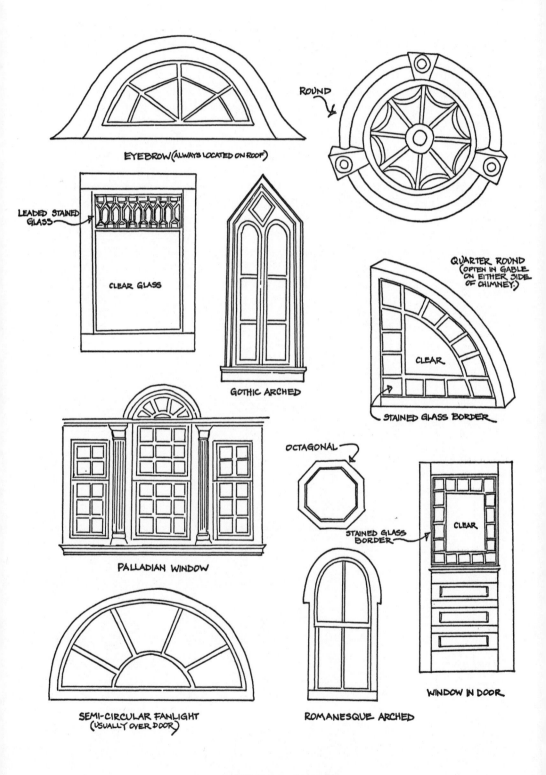

EYEBROW (ALWAYS LOCATED ON ROOF)

ROUND

LEADED STAINED GLASS

CLEAR GLASS

GOTHIC ARCHED

QUARTER ROUND (OFTEN IN GABLE ON EITHER SIDE OF CHIMNEY.)

CLEAR

STAINED GLASS BORDER

PALLADIAN WINDOW

OCTAGONAL

STAINED GLASS BORDER

CLEAR

WINDOW IN DOOR

SEMI-CIRCULAR FANLIGHT (USUALLY OVER DOOR)

ROMANESQUE ARCHED

A multiplicity of windows

The most popular window during the whole 18th century was that formed by a fixed (unmovable) top sash of nine, twelve, or more lights (panes of glass) over a movable lower sash of six, eight, or twelve. When the bottom sash was raised, it had to be held open with a stick or peg. The number of lights in both top and bottom sash was reduced to six during the first half of the 19th century, resulting in the extremely popular window known as a six over six (still manufactured in limited quantities today). As early glassmaking techniques imposed a limit on the size of pane that could be produced, it's usually true that the larger the lights, the more recent the sash. Glass with noticeable bubbles and waviness would also indicate manufacture prior to around 1850.

Although Palladian windows had been in vogue as early as the last half of the 18th century, it wasn't until the closing decades of the 19th century that ornamental windows came into their own. This period saw the introduction of a multiplicity of new shapes and sizes to match the imaginative forms of Victorian houses. Round, diamond-shaped, quatrefoil (four petals or leaves), and octagonal windows came into popularity at this time. Eyebrow windows seemed to raise themselves above the roofs of some houses, while Gothic and Romanesque

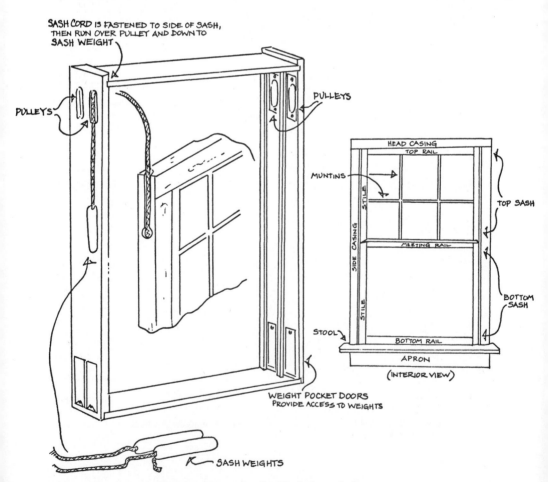

The anatomy of a double-hung window

arched casements peered out of the bays or towers of others. Stained, etched, and beveled glass often adorned already elegant windows, each house seemingly vying with its neighbors for the uniqueness of its fenestration (the arrangement and design of the windows and doors in a building).

The 18th-century double-sash window nevertheless survived all these innovations, although in a form improved by 19th-century technology. Both upper and lower sash of this window now became movable, through the use of ingeniously devised counterweights that moved up and down in concealed pockets. These double-hung windows are still popular today, although their counterweights have recently been replaced with friction slides.

If you have double-hung windows in your old-house that guillotine down of their own accord, you will have to replace their sash cord or chain. This is knotted or nailed in a groove in each side of the sash, run up over a pulley mounted at the top of the window jamb and down inside the weight pocket, where it's attached to a cast iron (or sometimes lead) counterweight. This is easily accessible through a little door hidden in the bottom of the jamb, which may be opened by the removal of one screw. In order to expose this door, however, you will first have to remove the window stop, lower sash, and parting strip. Once you have opened the weight pocket door, you will be able to drop a new cord or chain over the pulley and into the pocket, where you may snag it with a hook made from a coat hanger and pull it down to the weight.

Much of the charm of many old-house exteriors is contributed by the shutters or blinds that grace its windows, keeping them from staring wide-eyed at the world. Batten shutters were the first to be used in this country but were succeeded by the paneled variety as early as 1700. These gave way to fixed louver blinds toward the end of the 18th century, which in turn were superseded by blinds with movable louvers in the early 19th century.

If you add shutters or blinds to your old-house, be sure to match their style with the age of the building and to hang them so that they are functional as well as decorative. Never use ones too big or small for their windows and never consider (as I'm sure you wouldn't) the plastic or aluminum imitations that have recently come on the market! If you can't find suitable shutters or blinds for your old-house, it's far better to leave them off entirely.

You should be extremely reluctant to tear out the original windows and doors of your old-house and replace them with modern equivalents, even if they are in need of repair or seem wasteful of energy. Usually the cheapest and always the most authentic alternative is for you to recondition your old sash and doors (or find exact replacements if they are truly irredeemable—see Appendix), adding wooden storm doors and windows where necessary.

You should also carefully weigh the effects of any alteration to the existing configuration of the doors and windows of your old-house. It's often a great temptation to move them about to suit your individual use of the building, but be sure before you do so that it won't damage the architectural integrity of your

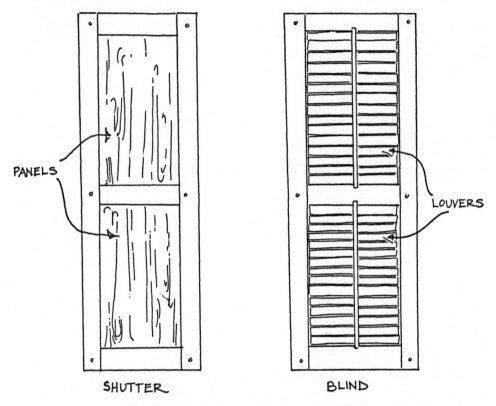

PANELS

LOUVERS

SHUTTER   BLIND

The difference between a shutter and a blind

house. This advice is curiously echoed (although in a far more alarming manner) by an early American superstition that warns us never to cut a new door in our old-house or to make a window out of an existing one or a member of our family is sure to die within the year!

CHAPTER

8

The Nervous System: Electricity in Your Old-House

When Frank Lloyd Wright remarked that "Bowels, circulation, and nerves were new in buildings" (of the late 19th century), he referred to the drainage, water supply, and electrical systems that were beginning to be installed in homes of that vintage. Although a few houses had rudimentary doorbell circuits in the early part of the century, it wasn't until after Thomas Edison had invented the incandescent light and activated the first electrical power station in New York City during the 1880s that a house could truly be said to have an electrical system.

Such early wiring was minimal and was executed by today's standards in an incredibly haphazard manner. It wasn't uncommon during this period to plaster directly over wires in walls and ceiling. The lime in the plaster would eat through the wires' thin insulation in a few years, causing short circuits and fires that destroyed many homes. Such practices produced increasing concern on the part of municipal authorities and insurance companies, leading to the publication in 1893 of the first edition of the National Electrical Code (NEC), which provided guidelines for what was then considered to be good wiring practice.

A wealth of electrical appliances were patented around the turn of the century, including the electric fan, sewing machine, hot plate, toaster, and clock. Although these were at first considered novelties, they had attained the status of necessities by the 1920s, along with the more recently developed electric stove, refrigerator, and washing machine. The curve of electrical power consumption has been sweeping dramatically upward from that time until the present, with its dangerous dependence on household electricity.

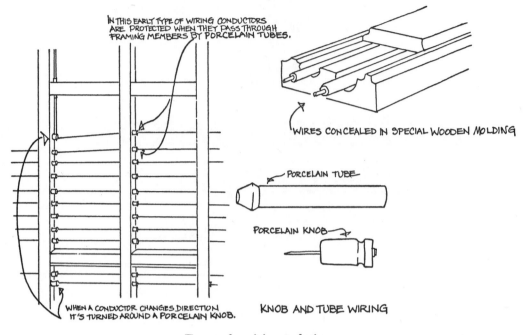

IN THIS EARLY TYPE OF WIRING CONDUCTORS ARE PROTECTED WHEN THEY PASS THROUGH FRAMING MEMBERS BY PORCELAIN TUBES.

WIRES CONCEALED IN SPECIAL WOODEN MOLDING

PORCELAIN TUBE

PORCELAIN KNOB

WHEN A CONDUCTOR CHANGES DIRECTION IT'S TURNED AROUND A PORCELAIN KNOB.

KNOB AND TUBE WIRING

Two early wiring techniques

Most old-houses were thus not originally designed to accommodate electrical systems at all and those that were are certainly ill-equipped to handle the volume of power we require today. It's therefore never possible to restore an old-house electrical system—you must renovate it, taking care that the new work is as unobtrusive as possible.

It's never legally obligatory to bring old-house wiring up to date, no matter how inadequate or dangerous it may be. Once you voluntarily decide to upgrade your wiring, however, your work must conform to the current National Electrical Code. Copies of this code may be obtained at electrical supply houses, but the text of the oracle is unfortunately almost incomprehensible. It's therefore worthwhile to procure one of the considerably more expensive *interpreted* versions of the code, at least one of which is actually quite lucid. (See McPartland in the Bibliography.)

You may wire your own home in most rural areas of the nation, provided only that your work passes an inspection given by a member of the Fire Underwriters to verify your compliance with the NEC. It's nevertheless more than likely that if you are a city dweller, you will require a license to do the same work. This requirement may sometimes be circumvented by making an agreement with a locally licensed electrician, whereby you technically act as his assistant. He will inspect your work and apply for approval by the Underwriters, thereby satisfying the municipal authorities even though you may have actually wired your house.

Despite the fact that you may be legally permitted to renovate the wiring

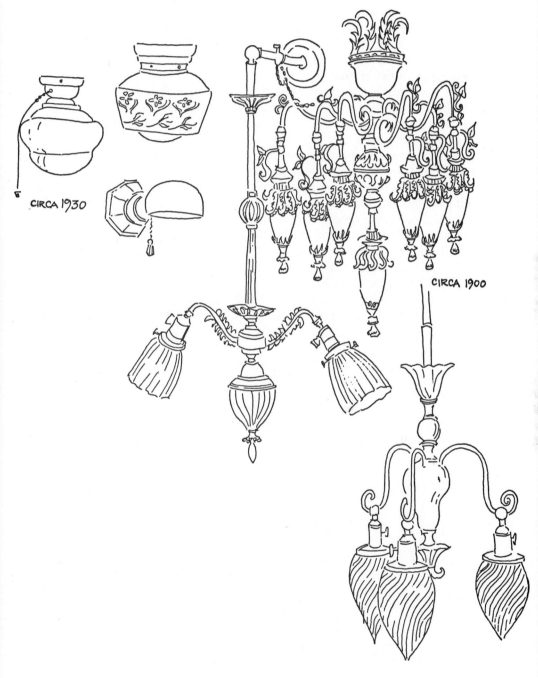

CIRCA 1930

CIRCA 1900

Period electrical fixtures may be rewired and retained.

system in your house, always bear in mind that it can be a hazardous occupation for both yourself and your home. Electricity should always have your highest respect, for it can on occasion prove to be a silent, invisible, and incredibly swift enemy that can kill you or burn your house to the ground with little regard for your feelings in the matter.

The most important component in your old-house's electrical system is its overload protection panel, for it's here that the building is protected from the awesome destructive power of electrical malfunction. If your house hasn't been rewired relatively recently, this will take the form of a metal or metal-lined wooden fuse box. The chances are that this will be crammed full of wires and surrounded by subsidiary boxes and switches, like moons around a planet. This overcrowded and complicated situation evolved as a multitude of appliances were added over the years to the electrical load of the house.

The thickest conductors (wires) entering the central fuse box, through a pipe known as a conduit or enclosed in a heavy cable of an inch or more in diameter, are called the service entrance conductors. The number of these determines the available voltages, while their diameters determine the amperage (electrical current) supplied to your house.

If there are only two conductors, the bare or white one will be neutral or non-voltage-carrying, while the black one will be "hot," with a voltage between itself and the neutral of 120 volts. If there is a third service entrance conductor, it

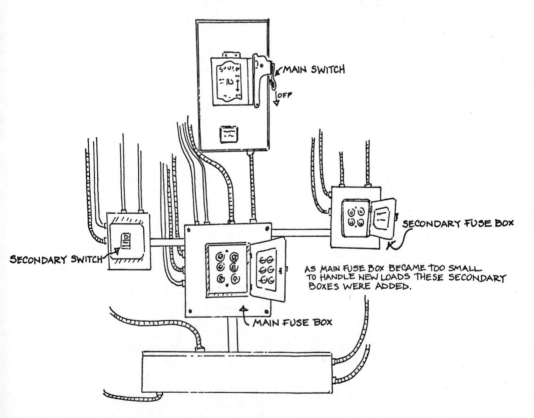

Old fuse box and its "moons"

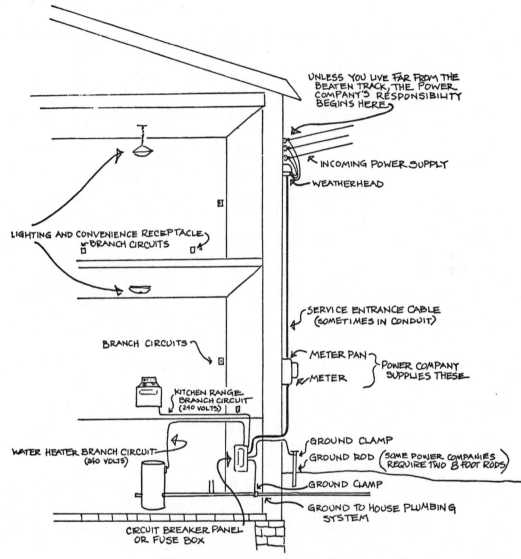

The anatomy of a house's electrical system

will be red and will have the same voltage between itself and neutral as does the black, yet will have a voltage of 240 volts with the black. Most of the old two-conductor services have long since been replaced, as they don't supply the requisite voltage for such common appliances as electric water heaters, ranges, or clothes dryers, but you may still encounter them occasionally. (The power to my typewriter is at this very moment supplied by such a service.)

The greater the diameter of the service entrance conductors, the greater their

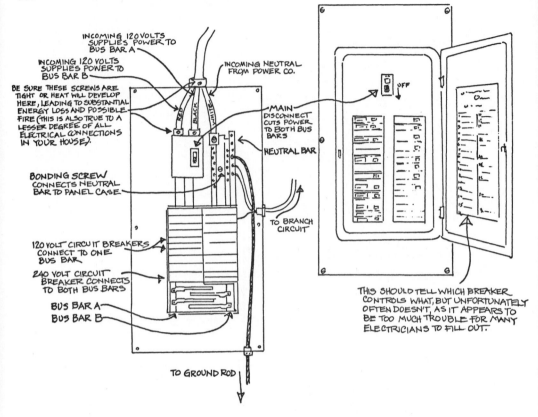

INCOMING 120 VOLTS SUPPLIES POWER TO BUS BAR A

INCOMING 120 VOLTS SUPPLIES POWER TO BUS BAR B

BE SURE THESE SCREWS ARE TIGHT OR HEAT WILL DEVELOP HERE, LEADING TO SUBSTANTIAL ENERGY LOSS AND POSSIBLE FIRE (THIS IS ALSO TRUE TO A LESSER DEGREE OF ALL ELECTRICAL CONNECTIONS IN YOUR HOUSE).

INCOMING NEUTRAL FROM POWER CO.

MAIN DISCONNECT CUTS POWER TO BOTH BUS BARS

NEUTRAL BAR

BONDING SCREW CONNECTS NEUTRAL BAR TO PANEL CASE.

120 VOLT CIRCUIT BREAKERS CONNECT TO ONE BUS BAR

240 VOLT CIRCUIT BREAKER CONNECTS TO BOTH BUS BARS

BUS BAR A
BUS BAR B

TO BRANCH CIRCUIT

THIS SHOULD TELL WHICH BREAKER CONTROLS WHAT, BUT UNFORTUNATELY OFTEN DOESN'T, AS IT APPEARS TO BE TOO MUCH TROUBLE FOR MANY ELECTRICIANS TO FILL OUT.

TO GROUND ROD

The anatomy of a circuit breaker panel

ampacity, or ability to conduct current. If yours are slightly more than ³⁄₁₆″ in diameter (not including the insulation), you have a 60 amp (ampere) service. This was at one time more than sufficient power for your house, but is definitely inadequate by today's standards.

One other very important wire enters your fuse box and is electrically connected to the neutral. This is known as the grounding conductor and doesn't originate at the power station but at a pipe or ground rod driven in the earth outside your house or at a ground clamp on the cold water supply of your plumbing system. This method of grounding ensures that for safety reasons there is never a voltage between the neutral and any part of your house except the black and red conductors supplied by the power company.

The neutral, black, and red conductors provide the source of your household power supply. All the electrical wiring in your house radiates outward from the service entrance, like nerves from the spinal cord. Every lighting fixture and receptacle (plug-in outlet) is fed from this point, being grouped in subdivisions of ten or twelve known as branch circuits. Certain heavy power consuming appliances, such as water heaters, dryers, ranges, freezers, and air conditioners have separate branch circuits to themselves, often at 240 volts.

The critical connections between the incoming conductors and outgoing branch circuits are protected in the older systems by a fuse box with heat-sensitive plug fuses, which can disconnect an overheated (overloaded) circuit from its incoming power. Each branch circuit is protected by its own plug fuse and all of them are collectively protected by a main cartridge fuse and manual switch.

If your service entrance conductors are less than ¼" in diameter without their insulation (indicating a less than 100 amp service) or are only two in number (indicating a lack of 240 volt potential), they should be replaced with three new ones rated to carry a load of from 100 to 200 amps (depending on the size of your house and your probable consumption of power). You should also take this opportunity to replace your crowded fuse box with a circuit breaker panel that has the same rating as your new service entrance conductors. Circuit breakers are merely heat-sensitive switches that accomplish exactly the same end as fuses, but are far more convenient, as they need only to be reset rather than replaced after being tripped by an overload.

The installation of your service entrance conductors and panel can be dangerous and is subject to a host of NEC regulations. You might be well advised to make this the part of the job that you offer as bait to a licensed electrician, so that he might consider letting you wire the rest of your house under his license.

Now that your old-house has a new service entrance and panel, you may be confident that you have enough power available to safely add any wiring you might desire and that the existing wiring is adequately protected in case of overload or short circuit. Before you begin to add new branch circuits or rejuvenate old ones, however, there are a number of provisions of the NEC you should familiarize yourself with.

The lighting fixtures and receptacles in living rooms, halls, and bedrooms must be grouped into lighting branch circuits of from eight to twelve outlets, employing a minimum of #14 wire (this has a diameter of .0641") and must be protected by a 15 amp circuit breaker. The receptacles on these circuits must be so situated that no point on the perimeter of a room is more than 6' away from one. This will allow a lamp or appliance to be plugged in anywhere around the room without needing an extension cord.

Although kitchen lighting fixtures are included in one of the lighting circuits, kitchen receptacles are not. The code requires a minimum of two separate kitchen appliance circuits for these receptacles, which must be protected with 20 amp breakers and run with #12 wire (this has a diameter of .0808"—illogically enough, the larger the number of the wire, the smaller its diameter). These circuits are very logically required to handle the heavy electrical demand imposed by many of the small appliances commonly used in the kitchen, such as toasters, fryers, broilers, and irons.

The bathroom normally only requires one receptacle, yet this must be on a special ground fault interrupter (GFI) circuit, along with any receptacles on the outside of your house. This circuit employs a special breaker or receptacle that obviates the possibility of serious electrical shock in these hazardous areas by switching off the circuit should there be the slightest flow of current from the "hot" wire to ground. Thus if your radio suddenly decides to take a bath with you (an occurrence that has killed quite a number of people over the years), the power would shut off before you felt more than a tingle.

Electric water heaters, pumps, kitchen ranges, air conditioners, freezers, and clothes dryers all must have special branch circuits of their own, utilizing wire and breakers commensurate with their individual power ratings. These are expressed in watts (amps times volts) and may not exceed 80 percent of the capacity of their circuit. A 5500 watt water heater drawing nearly 23 amps at 240 volts must therefore be fused with a 30 amp breaker and connected to the panel with #10 wire (80 percent of 30 amps = 24 amps, representing the maximum current draw permissible in that circuit).

Let's assume that you blow a fuse every time you simultaneously put bread in your toaster and brew coffee in your electric percolator. As having toast and coffee at the same time doesn't seem too much to ask, you decide to add a kitchen appliance circuit to the wiring system of your old-house. You know you must run #12 wire from your kitchen to the fuse box or panel in the basement and that the circuit must be protected with a 20 amp fuse or breaker. But how do you actually accomplish this?

You may begin by locating the positions of the new receptacles to be included in the circuit and by cutting holes in the wall for them. These must be placed so as to conform to the same rule applying to convenience receptacles, but you must install at least one additional one over every kitchen counter-top wider than a foot. Mark the holes with a 2" × 3" × 3½" deep device box (the metal or plastic box to which you will later secure a receptacle) as a template, taking care not to locate any of them over a stud. You must cut these holes very gently if your walls are plaster, in order not to disturb its key with the lath.

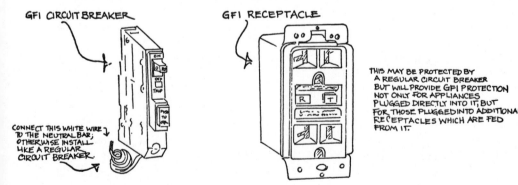

A ground fault interrupter (GFI) will protect a circuit so that it's virtually impossible to receive a shock from an appliance connected to it.

TO CUT A HOLE FOR A DEVICE OR SWITCH BOX IN A PLASTER WALL, FIRST CAREFULLY CHIP AWAY PLASTER WITH CHISEL OR SCREWDRIVER, THEN

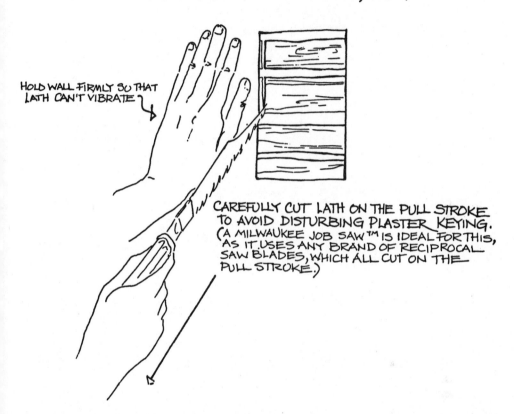

HOLD WALL FIRMLY SO THAT LATH CAN'T VIBRATE

CAREFULLY CUT LATH ON THE PULL STROKE TO AVOID DISTURBING PLASTER KEYING. (A MILWAUKEE JOB SAW™ IS IDEAL FOR THIS, AS IT USES ANY BRAND OF RECIPROCAL SAW BLADES, WHICH ALL CUT ON THE PULL STROKE.)

You must now run a cable (two or more conductors enclosed in a protective sheath) from one of the holes you have made to the panel. If local codes permit (they don't in New York City), use Romex or plastic-sheathed, rather than BX or metal-sheathed cable, as it's much easier to work with and is perfectly acceptable according to the NEC. (Unless your house is infested with rats or mice, which will on occasion try to bite through these cables.) Cables are firstly described by the gauge (thickness) and secondly by the number of the insulated conductors they carry (the bare grounding conductor doesn't count). The cable you will need in this particular instance is thus known as 12-2 Romex and contains three wires: white (neutral), black ("hot"), and bare (ground).

Routing cables through an old-house can be challenging, but the knowledge you have earlier acquired of its construction should make the job easier. Always follow the path of least resistance, utilizing where possible such easy routes as may be provided by unfinished cellar ceilings and attic floors, disused air or dumbwaiter shafts, pipe chases, or voids around chimneys. Cables may also be

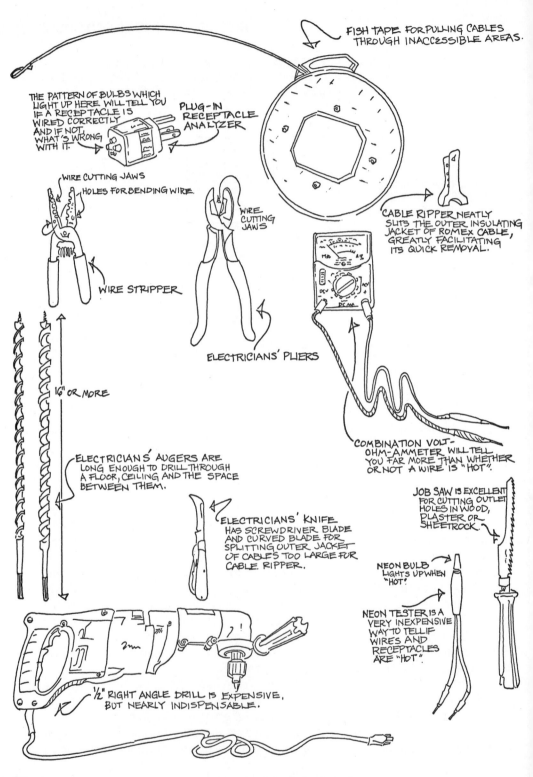

FISH TAPE FOR PULLING CABLES THROUGH INACCESSIBLE AREAS.

THE PATTERN OF BULBS WHICH LIGHT UP HERE WILL TELL YOU IF A RECEPTACLE IS WIRED CORRECTLY AND IF NOT, WHAT'S WRONG WITH IT.

PLUG-IN RECEPTACLE ANALYZER

WIRE CUTTING JAWS

HOLES FOR BENDING WIRE.

WIRE CUTTING JAWS

CABLE RIPPER NEATLY SLITS THE OUTER INSULATING JACKET OF ROMEX CABLE, GREATLY FACILITATING ITS QUICK REMOVAL.

WIRE STRIPPER

ELECTRICIANS' PLIERS

16" OR MORE

ELECTRICIAN'S AUGERS ARE LONG ENOUGH TO DRILL THROUGH A FLOOR, CEILING AND THE SPACE BETWEEN THEM.

COMBINATION VOLT-OHM-AMMETER WILL TELL YOU FAR MORE THAN WHETHER OR NOT A WIRE IS "HOT".

JOB SAW IS EXCELLENT FOR CUTTING OUTLET HOLES IN WOOD, PLASTER OR SHEETROCK.

ELECTRICIANS' KNIFE HAS SCREWDRIVER BLADE AND CURVED BLADE FOR SPLITTING OUTER JACKET OF CABLES TOO LARGE FOR CABLE RIPPER.

NEON BULB LIGHTS UP WHEN "HOT".

NEON TESTER IS A VERY INEXPENSIVE WAY TO TELL IF WIRES AND RECEPTACLES ARE "HOT".

½" RIGHT ANGLE DRILL IS EXPENSIVE, BUT NEARLY INDISPENSABLE.

An electrician's basic tools

conveniently concealed for short distances behind previously removed trim and baseboards.

Let's assume in this particular case that the panel is located in the cellar, which has an unfinished ceiling. You may then drill a 1" hole up through the ceiling at the point directly beneath the proposed receptacle nearest to the panel (this may be ascertained by accurate measurement from some kitchen landmark, such as a waste or vent pipe). Now insert the end of an electrician's fish tape in the hole you have bored and push it upward while your wife, husband, or friend (who chances to be preparing dinner in the kitchen above) watches, listens, and feels for it to appear at the appropriate hole in the wall.

Once your helper has securely taped the end of a coil of 12-2 Romex to the end of the fish tape, you may pull the cable through the wall into the cellar and on to the panel. (You may have to bore holes in intervening floor joists, through which it may pass.) You must now run a cable from the same hole in the wall to the next box location, from that to the third, and so on to the last. Unless the kitchen walls are open in places or it's easy to remove a baseboard, it will probably be easier for you to route each of these cables down to the cellar and back up again.

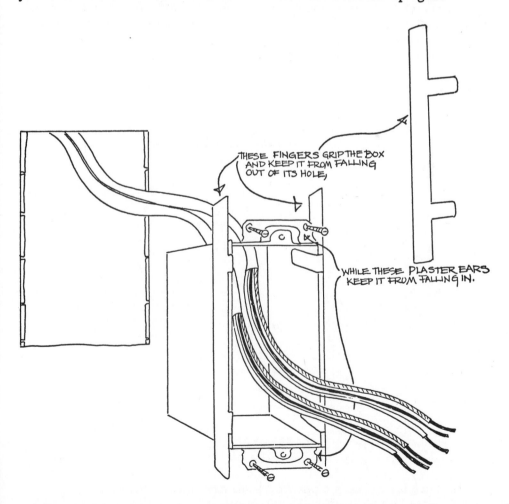

THESE FINGERS GRIP THE BOX AND KEEP IT FROM FALLING OUT OF ITS HOLE,

WHILE THESE PLASTER EARS KEEP IT FROM FALLING IN.

When you have connected every hole and run a wire from one of them to the panel (leave at least 1' of cable hanging out at each hole and 6' at the panel), you are ready to install device boxes in each hole. Strip about 10" of the outer insulation off each cable with a cable ripper and electrician's pliers, pry out the appropriate number of knock outs in each device box, and insert the cables in the resultant holes. If you are using metal boxes, each cable must pass through a Romex connector or internal cable clamp where it enters the box, which must be tightened after it has passed through. (Romex may enter plastic boxes with no such connectors or clamps.)

The device boxes may now be secured to the wall with an ingenious combination of plaster ears and fingers, the first of which keeps the box from falling into the hole and the second from falling out. The ears come attached to certain boxes, but the fingers must be slipped in the hole alongside the box as it's inserted and their tabs bent into it.

Once all the boxes are secured to the walls, you may proceed to install the receptacles. Start by screwing a 1' long piece of bare #12 wire to a tapped hole in the back of each box by means of a ground screw. Now twist all the bare wires together in each box, slip a ground ferrule over them and crimp it with a special crimping tool or electrician's pliers. One of these wires may be connected to the green screw on the receptacle and the others may be cut off near the ferrule.

Next strip about ⅝" of insulation from the ends of all black and white conductors with a wire stripper and bend each bare end into a curved hook by means of the small hole in the stripper. Now attach the white wires to the

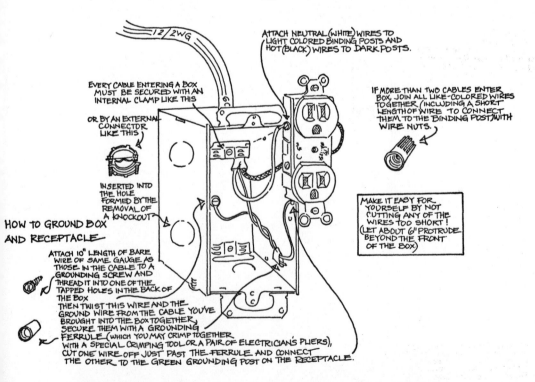

How to bring a cable into a device box and how to wire a receptacle

light-colored receptacle binding screws and the black wires to the dark-colored ones, making sure that the hook is placed over them so as to make it close rather than open as the screw is tightened down. If there are more than two of the same color conductors in a box, twist them together with a short length of the same color wire, secure the joint with a Wire Nut and tape and connect the short wire to the receptacle. This may now be secured to its box with the two screws provided and a duplex cover plate fastened to it.

The very last step in wiring a circuit should be to connect it to the panel, for obvious (yet often overlooked) safety reasons. After bringing the stripped cable into the panel through a Romex connector, secure the bare and white wires to the neutral bar. (This will be readily identifiable as both the grounding conductor and the neutral service entrance conductor will be fastened to it, as well as all the bare and white wires from any other circuits that enter the panel.) You may now secure the black wire to the binding post of a 20 amp breaker (of the same make as the panel) and snap it into position on the bus bar running down the center of the panel. Turn the breaker into the "on" position and check your new receptacles with a receptacle tester. If the two yellow lights go on, your circuit is a success!

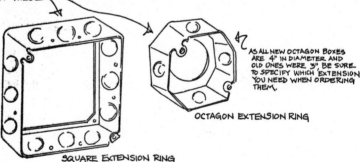

IF YOU'RE FORCED TO BRING MORE WIRES INTO A BOX THAN IT CAN ACCOMODATE (ALTHOUGH SUCH OVERCROWDING IS OFTEN OBVIOUS, THE NEC HAS STRICT RULES FOR THIS SITUATION, LISTED IN TABLE 370-6 [9]), YOU MAY SOMETIMES BE ABLE TO MAKE THE BOX LARGE ENOUGH BY ADDING ONE OF THESE.

AS ALL NEW OCTAGON BOXES ARE 4" IN DIAMETER AND OLD ONES WERE 3", BE SURE TO SPECIFY WHICH EXTENSION YOU NEED WHEN ORDERING THEM.

OCTAGON EXTENSION RING

SQUARE EXTENSION RING

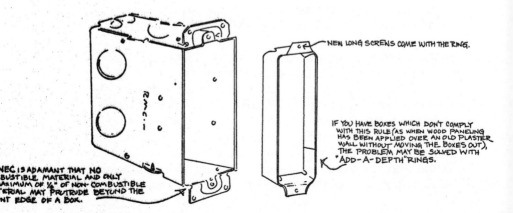

NEW LONG SCREWS COME WITH THE RING.

IF YOU HAVE BOXES WHICH DON'T COMPLY WITH THIS RULE (AS WHEN WOOD PANELING HAS BEEN APPLIED OVER AN OLD PLASTER WALL WITHOUT MOVING THE BOXES OUT), THE PROBLEM MAY BE SOLVED WITH "ADD-A-DEPTH" RINGS.

THE NEC IS ADAMANT THAT NO COMBUSTIBLE MATERIAL AND ONLY A MAXIMUM OF ¼" OF NON-COMBUSTIBLE MATERIAL MAY PROTRUDE BEYOND THE FRONT EDGE OF A BOX.

9

The Circulatory and Excretory Systems: Water Supply and Waste Disposal

No part of an old-house's anatomy is viewed with such a peculiar mixture of humor, distaste, and fascination as is its plumbing system. This unusual attitude is undoubtedly a product of our perception of the correspondence between it and the less mentionable portions of our own anatomies. It's therefore not surprising that the history of plumbing has long been treated with lamentable jocularity, making it extremely difficult to be sure exactly when it was introduced into the first American home.

George Vanderbilt probably has the best-authenticated honor of this claim, enjoying the privileges afforded by indoor water closet (toilet), tub, and lavatory (bathroom sink) in his New York City mansion as early as 1855. Such luxuries remained the nearly exclusive acquisitions of the affluent for nearly half a century, for they were at that time hardly considered essential for human well-being. Frequent bathing was indeed vehemently opposed by many doctors of the time on the grounds that it could prove injurious to one's health!

Although the Vanderbilt bathroom was really quite plain, its successors as the Victorian era burst into full flower became increasingly elegant and ornate. Plumbing fixtures came eventually to more closely resemble fine pieces of furniture than they did utilitarian devices designed to promote health and cleanliness. Tubs and lavatories were commonly enclosed with elaborate hardwood paneling, lavatory tops were fashioned of marble inset with decorative porcelain bowls, and water closets were at times truly worthy of the euphemism "throne."

The Victorian bathroom had nonetheless fallen into disrepute by the turn of the century, becoming the object of widespread censure for its ornate and unsanitary construction, which was thought to provide a breeding ground for pestilence and disease. Faulty and unsanitary household plumbing systems had suddenly become the scapegoats of all human ills. A tract of the day entitled *Women, Plumbers and Doctors* assures us that if "women and plumbers do their whole sanitary duty, there will be comparatively little occasion for the services of doctors." This climate of opinion not only revolutionized bathroom design, but changed its status from that of a luxury affordable only by the Vanderbilts of the world to that of a household necessity.

The turn-of-the-century bathroom was sanitary above all, with white tiled floors and white vitreous china or enameled cast iron fixtures. These sometimes included such exotic items as foot baths, *sitz* baths (for sitting in), and *rain baths* (as showers were first called), as well as the usual tub, lavatory, and water closet. As the philosophy of the day called for scrupulous scrubbing and scouring of all these fixtures' surfaces (as well as those of our own bodies), they were freestanding,

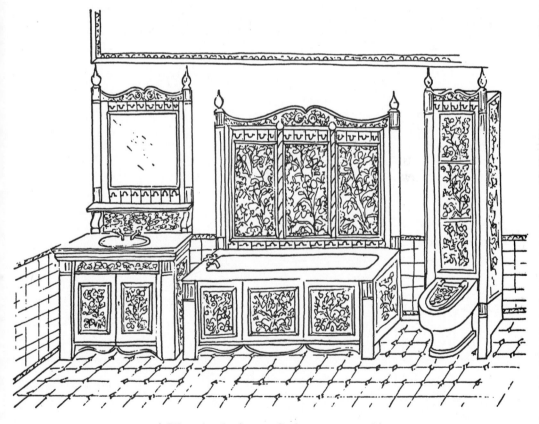

A Victorian bathroom fit for a queen or king

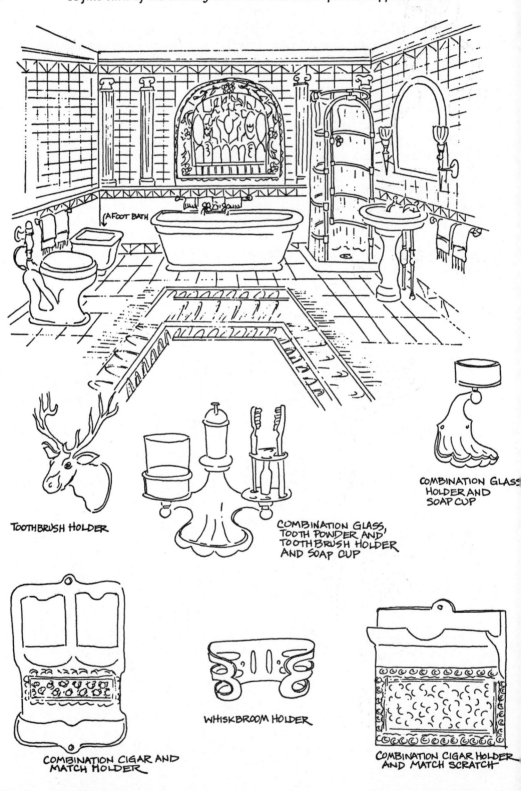

A fine turn of the century bathroom with some possible appurtenances

(A FOOT BATH)

TOOTHBRUSH HOLDER

COMBINATION GLASS, TOOTH POWDER AND TOOTHBRUSH HOLDER AND SOAP CUP

COMBINATION GLASS HOLDER AND SOAP CUP

COMBINATION CIGAR AND MATCH HOLDER

WHISKBROOM HOLDER

COMBINATION CIGAR HOLDER AND MATCH SCRATCH

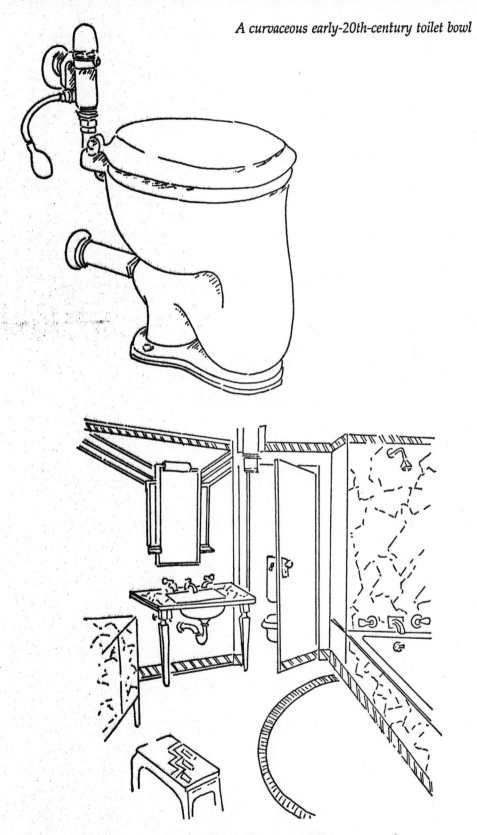

A curveaceous early-20th-century toilet bowl

Art deco bathroom c. 1930

curvaceous, and conspicuously lacking in cracks and crevices in which dirt might lodge.

The foot and sitz baths had gone the way of razor strops and spittoons by the 1930s and the remaining fixtures had become more angular due to the art deco influence of the 1920s. Sanitary standards had relaxed enough by the middle of the 20th century to permit lavatories, tubs, and toilets to assume a variety of colors in addition to hygienic white. Tubs were once again allowed to hug the walls and lavatories to be enclosed in pieces of furniture, now called vanities (although comparison with their Victorian counterparts certainly isn't flattering).

If you're fortunate enough to have an old-house with period bathroom fixtures, make every effort to preserve them, for they may have great distinction and their loss would greatly diminish the authenticity of your bathroom. If the enamel on your tub or lavatory is worn, chipped, or badly stained, it may be

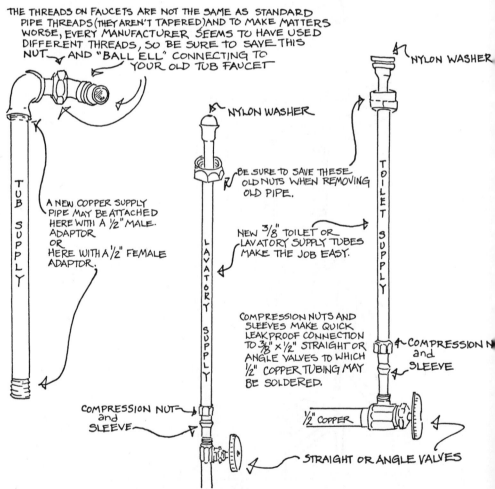

How to connect new pipe to old fixtures

rejuvenated without removal of the fixture. This isn't something you can do yourself, but there are specialists in this kind of restoration in most areas of the country and while their services may not be cheap, they will undoubtedly be less expensive than replacing the fixture. If your fixtures are leaky, you may usually fix them yourself with but minimum outlay for materials, as almost all such leaks are caused by the deterioration of inexpensive gaskets or washers. The replacement of some of these is extremely easy, while others require considerable time and patience.

The water supplied to your fixtures should have an operating pressure of around forty pounds per square inch, almost always produced by a pump. This need not concern you if you live in a community with a municipal water supply, but if you're a country dweller, your supply system probably includes a pump and pressure tank. The pump is quite literally the heart of your system, but as there are

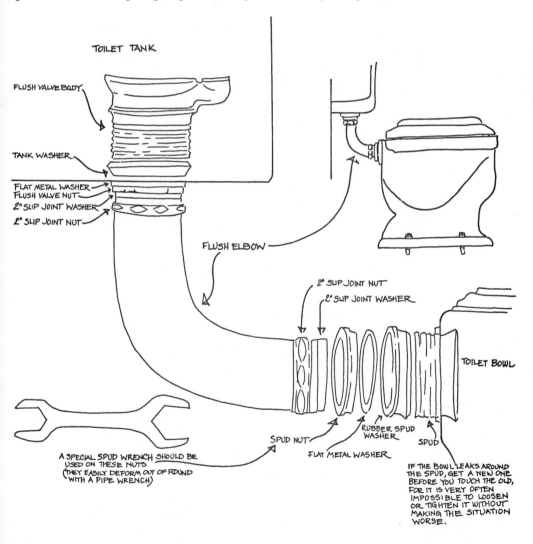

The anatomy of the often troublesome joint between tank and bowl of early toilets

many different kinds of them and some of these are quite complicated, you should leave open heart surgery to the professional.

If your pump continually shuts off and then on again, however, it may not be the fault of the pump at all and may therefore be the province of the amateur. This symptom may be caused by a defective foot valve or check valve, both of which are designed to permit water to pass from the well to the pressure tank, but not back again. (The foot valve is located at the bottom of the well, while the check valve is on the inlet side of the pump.) If one of these valves leaks water back to the well, it will cause the pump to overwork itself and the defective valve should be replaced.

It's even more likely that the same symptom is caused by a waterlogged pressure tank, which has lost the essential cushion of air at its top. This may be

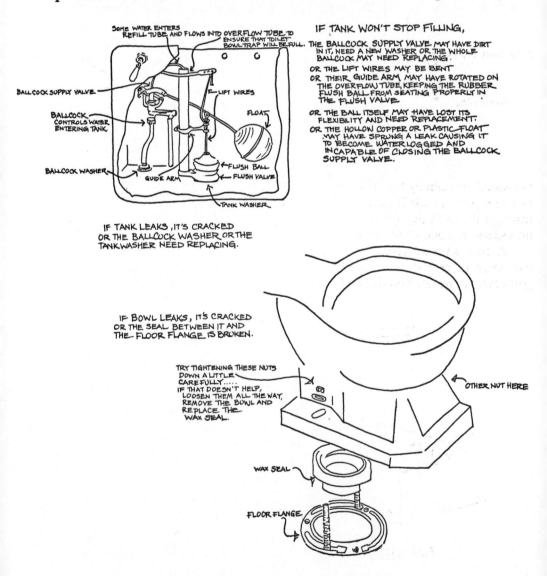

The pathology of the toilet tank and bowl

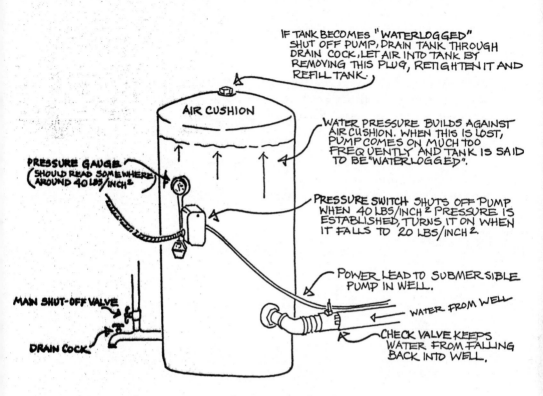

IF TANK BECOMES "WATERLOGGED" SHUT OFF PUMP, DRAIN TANK THROUGH DRAIN COCK, LET AIR INTO TANK BY REMOVING THIS PLUG, RETIGHTEN IT AND REFILL TANK.

AIR CUSHION

WATER PRESSURE BUILDS AGAINST AIR CUSHION. WHEN THIS IS LOST, PUMP COMES ON MUCH TOO FREQUENTLY AND TANK IS SAID TO BE "WATERLOGGED".

PRESSURE GAUGE (SHOULD READ SOMEWHERE AROUND 40 LBS/INCH²)

PRESSURE SWITCH SHUTS OFF PUMP WHEN 40 LBS/INCH² PRESSURE IS ESTABLISHED, TURNS IT ON WHEN IT FALLS TO 20 LBS/INCH².

POWER LEAD TO SUBMERSIBLE PUMP IN WELL.

MAIN SHUT-OFF VALVE

WATER FROM WELL

DRAIN COCK

CHECK VALVE KEEPS WATER FROM FALLING BACK INTO WELL.

A pressure tank

alleviated by draining the tank with the pump turned off and then refilling it. If the problem persists, air is escaping from around the plug at the top of the tank or through the air valve on its side. Tightening the first or lightly striking (or, if necessary, replacing) the second should cure the problem for good.

A main shut-off valve is located near the outlet of the pressure tank or near the water meter (the device that measures the amount of water you consume) if you have city water. You should be well acquainted with this valve's location, as it

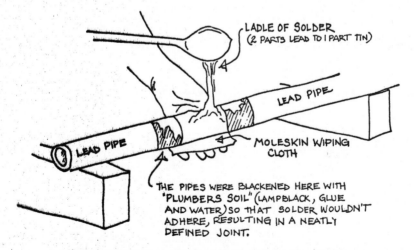

LADLE OF SOLDER (2 PARTS LEAD TO 1 PART TIN)

LEAD PIPE

LEAD PIPE

MOLESKIN WIPING CLOTH

THE PIPES WERE BLACKENED HERE WITH "PLUMBERS SOIL" (LAMPBLACK, GLUE AND WATER) SO THAT SOLDER WOULDN'T ADHERE, RESULTING IN A NEATLY DEFINED JOINT.

Two lead pipes used to be joined with a wiped joint.

controls your whole supply system, both cold and hot. How can a valve in the cold water supply shut off the hot water as well? Closing the main shut-off (which should be left wide open at other times) depressurizes the system from that point on: There is no pressure to drive water into the water heater and hence none to drive the hot water out.

The first extensively used supply piping was made of lead, but you are unlikely to encounter any as it has been largely replaced, due to its unfortunate habit of poisoning the water. Although lead poisoning was well known in the 19th

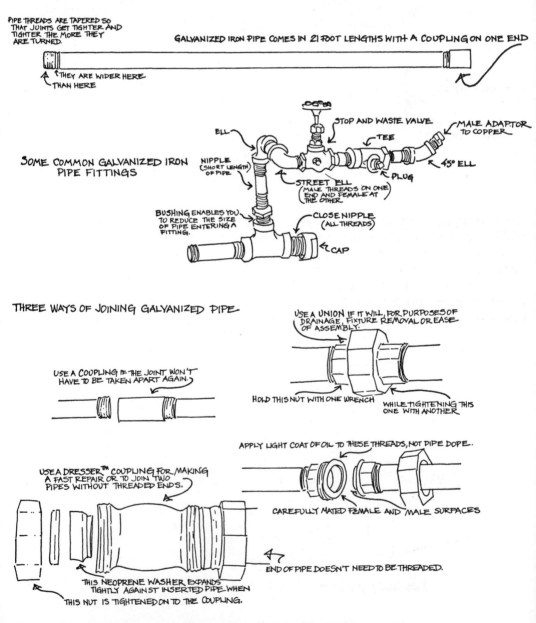

How to use galvanized iron pipe

century, it was believed that the nontoxic oxide which rapidly formed on a pipe's interior would protect the water from the lead. This appears to have been a correct assumption in most, but not *all* instances (such as those where the water is quite acidic or alkaline). Any such exceptions should make a strong enough case for you to replace any lead supply piping you may find in your old-house!

If your plumbing hasn't been recently modernized, it is more than likely that your supplies will be galvanized (zinc-coated) iron. These are strong, durable, and nontoxic, but gradually fill up with rust, which can reduce the inside diameter of a

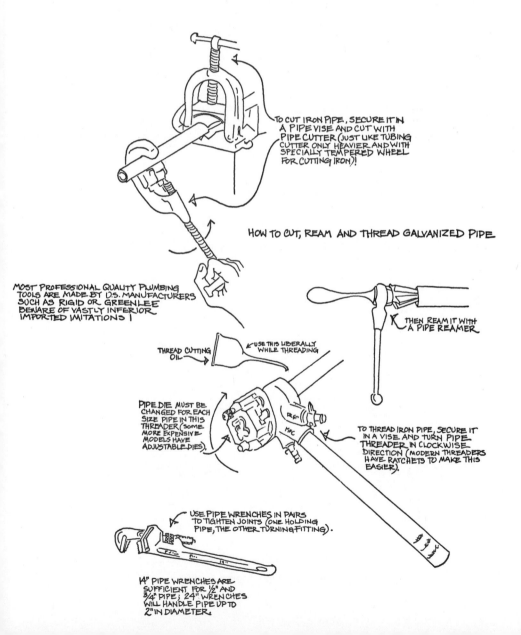

TO CUT IRON PIPE, SECURE IT IN A PIPE VISE AND CUT WITH PIPE CUTTER (JUST LIKE TUBING CUTTER ONLY HEAVIER AND WITH SPECIALLY TEMPERED WHEEL FOR CUTTING IRON)!

HOW TO CUT, REAM AND THREAD GALVANIZED PIPE

MOST PROFESSIONAL QUALITY PLUMBING TOOLS ARE MADE BY U.S. MANUFACTURERS SUCH AS RIGID OR GREENLEE. BEWARE OF VASTLY INFERIOR IMPORTED IMITATIONS!

THREAD CUTTING OIL →

USE THIS LIBERALLY WHILE THREADING

THEN REAM IT WITH A PIPE REAMER

PIPE DIE MUST BE CHANGED FOR EACH SIZE PIPE IN THIS THREADER (SOME MORE EXPENSIVE MODELS HAVE ADJUSTABLE DIES).

TO THREAD IRON PIPE, SECURE IT IN A VISE AND TURN PIPE THREADER IN CLOCKWISE DIRECTION (MODERN THREADERS HAVE RATCHETS TO MAKE THIS EASIER).

USE PIPE WRENCHES IN PAIRS TO TIGHTEN JOINTS (ONE HOLDING PIPE, THE OTHER TURNING FITTING).

14" PIPE WRENCHES ARE SUFFICIENT FOR 1/2" AND 3/4" PIPE; 24" WRENCHES WILL HANDLE PIPE UP TO 2" IN DIAMETER.

pipe over the course of several decades to the point at which the flow of water is impeded or stopped completely. As it's this crucial diameter that determines a pipe's capacity, all water pipes are designated by this dimension (a ¾" galvanized pipe will thus actually have an outside diameter of about 1").

If water barely manages to trickle through the rust-clogged pipes of your old-house, you should consider replacing its galvanized iron supply piping with type L rigid copper tubing. It's called "rigid" because it's difficult to bend without kinking, "type L" because it has a medium thickness wall (the thinner type M is used for low-pressure heating systems and the thicker type K for underground installation), and "tubing" instead of pipe for no better reason than rope is called

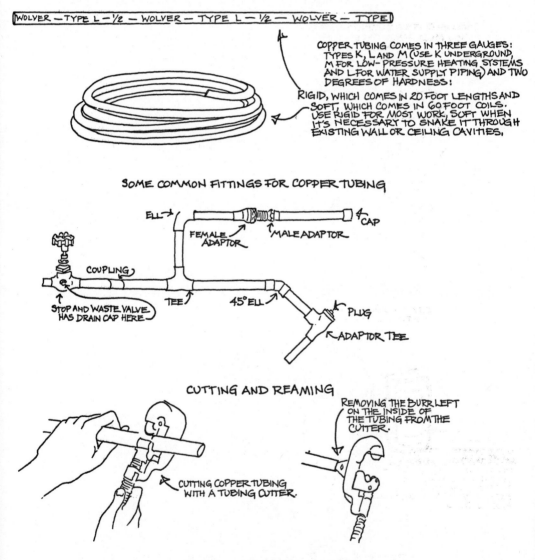

How to work with copper tubing

"line" on board ship. Type L flexible tubing is also available and may be used to great advantage in making vertical runs through existing walls. (It may be "fished" into position like a wire.) If used for long horizontal runs, it tends to sag and form objectionable "pockets" that will trap water when the system is drained.

Copper tubing is nontoxic, easy to work with, and relatively inexpensive in the diameters needed for your supply system. You may of course prefer to replace old galvanized pipe with new (or your local plumbing code may require it), but this will be considerably more work. PVC (polyvinyl chloride) tubing has been a less expensive alternative to copper for a number of years, but its possible toxicity and unaesthetic appearance more than offset the slight savings it effects.

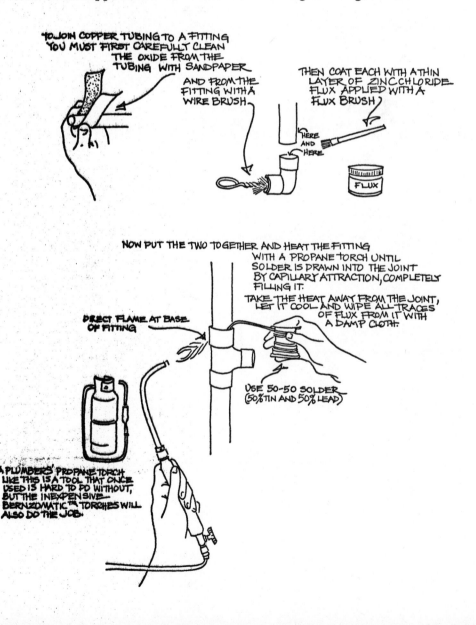

TO JOIN COPPER TUBING TO A FITTING YOU MUST FIRST CAREFULLY CLEAN THE OXIDE FROM THE TUBING WITH SANDPAPER

AND FROM THE FITTING WITH A WIRE BRUSH.

THEN COAT EACH WITH A THIN LAYER OF ZINC CHLORIDE FLUX APPLIED WITH A FLUX BRUSH

HERE AND HERE

FLUX

NOW PUT THE TWO TOGETHER AND HEAT THE FITTING WITH A PROPANE TORCH UNTIL SOLDER IS DRAWN INTO THE JOINT BY CAPILLARY ATTRACTION, COMPLETELY FILLING IT.

TAKE THE HEAT AWAY FROM THE JOINT, LET IT COOL AND WIPE ALL TRACES OF FLUX FROM IT WITH A DAMP CLOTH.

DIRECT FLAME AT BASE OF FITTING

USE 50-50 SOLDER (50% TIN AND 50% LEAD)

A PLUMBERS' PROPANE TORCH LIKE THIS IS A TOOL THAT ONCE USED IS HARD TO DO WITHOUT, BUT THE INEXPENSIVE BERNZOMATIC™ TORCHES WILL ALSO DO THE JOB.

Regardless of the kind of pipe used in your water supply system, there should be shut-off valves at each fixture and a pressure-temperature relief valve in the hot line at your water heater. The first make it possible to remove or repair an individual fixture without shutting the whole system down, while the latter prevents the possibility of an explosion due to malfunction of your water heater. It's also most important to be sure to always shut off the supply of power or fuel to a water heater before draining the water out of it.

An essential (although often overlooked) feature of a water supply system is that it be readily drainable for repair or in the eventuality that you wish to leave

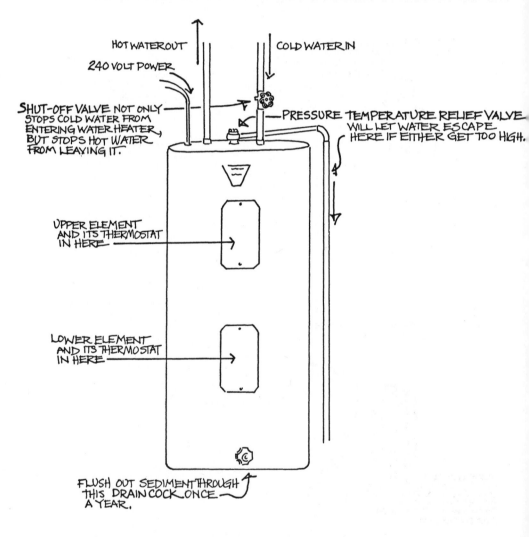

HOT WATER OUT   COLD WATER IN

240 VOLT POWER

SHUT-OFF VALVE NOT ONLY STOPS COLD WATER FROM ENTERING WATER HEATER, BUT STOPS HOT WATER FROM LEAVING IT.

PRESSURE TEMPERATURE RELIEF VALVE WILL LET WATER ESCAPE HERE IF EITHER GET TOO HIGH.

UPPER ELEMENT AND ITS THERMOSTAT IN HERE

LOWER ELEMENT AND ITS THERMOSTAT IN HERE

FLUSH OUT SEDIMENT THROUGH THIS DRAIN COCK ONCE A YEAR.

Electric water heater

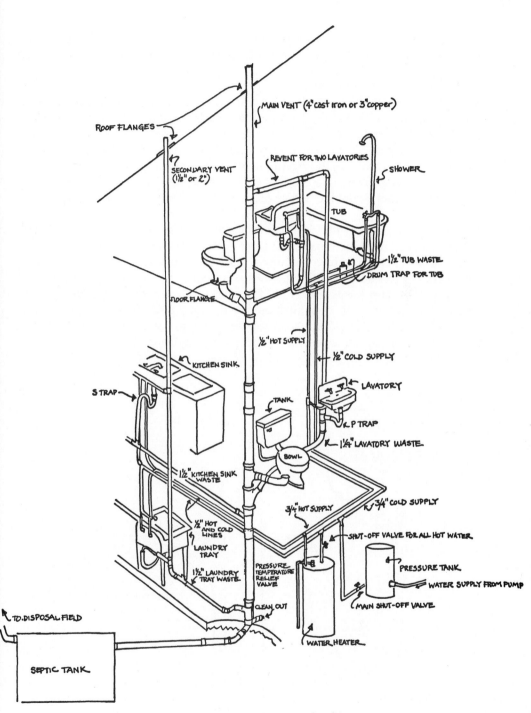

The anatomy of an old-house plumbing system

113

your house unheated during the winter months. This may be ensured by pitching all horizontal runs of pipe toward drain points with removable plugs or drain valves.

Each fixture must of course have provision for waste water to drain into the waste disposal system. This will eventually culminate in a 3″ or 4″ house drain that pitches at about ¼″ to the foot (as should all horizontal runs in the system) to the street sewer in a municipality or to the cesspool or septic tank in the country. A cesspool will probably be frowned upon by your local plumbing code, being nothing more than a pit in the ground in which raw sewage collects. A concrete or steel septic tank provides a system of baffles by which relatively clean effluent is separated from septic sludge, which must be periodically pumped out and hauled away.

During the turn-of-the-century obsession with sanitary practices, the arch villain was undoubtedly the waste disposal system, which allowed "sewer gas" to seep into the house and into the lungs of the unfortunate inhabitants. A host of incredibly complicated plumbing codes were consequently enacted to forestall the escape of this noxious enemy. Although sewer gas is no longer held responsible for most of the evils then attributed to it, many plumbing codes haven't yet adjusted to this fact. Their provisions for venting it to the outside air are therefore often incredibly complicated and unnecessarily rigorous.

Venting is accomplished by means of one or more vent stacks, which run

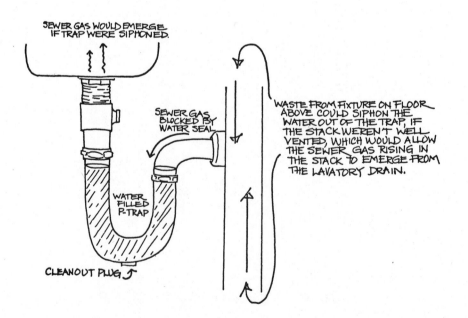

The function of a trap

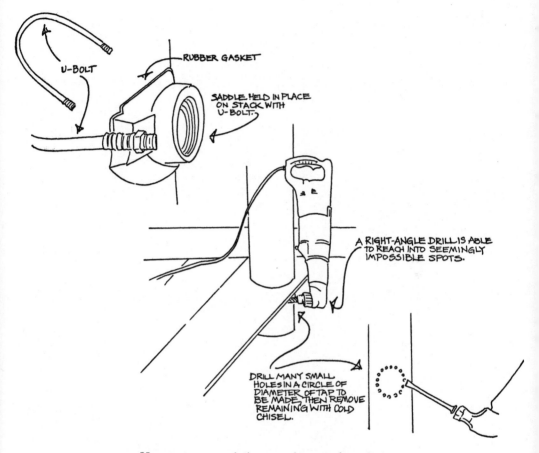

U-BOLT

RUBBER GASKET

SADDLE HELD IN PLACE ON STACK WITH U-BOLT.

A RIGHT-ANGLE DRILL IS ABLE TO REACH INTO SEEMINGLY IMPOSSIBLE SPOTS.

DRILL MANY SMALL HOLES IN A CIRCLE OF DIAMETER OF TAP TO BE MADE, THEN REMOVE REMAINING WITH COLD CHISEL.

How to tap an existing cast iron stack or drain

from the main horizontal waste line upward through the roof, where they dis-charge malodorous gas into the atmosphere. Some of this would nevertheless inevitably escape into the house through the fixture drains, if these weren't provided with traps. The familiar S- or P-shaped bends under lavatories and kitchen sinks aren't there to trap hair, grease, and an occasional diamond ring, but rather to trap water to act as barriers to the escape of sewer gas. Toilets have similar water traps built into their bowls, while tub and shower traps are hidden beneath the floor (sometimes accessible from above through a round brass plate).

If a fixture is too far away from the nearest vent stack, the water may be siphoned out of its trap when another fixture (usually the toilet) is used, thus allowing sewer gas to escape from its drain. It would be as difficult for this siphonage to occur in a well-vented system as it would be to siphon gas out of a car if the tube you are sucking on has a hole in it through which air may enter.

A good rule of thumb (although not recognized by some codes) for the

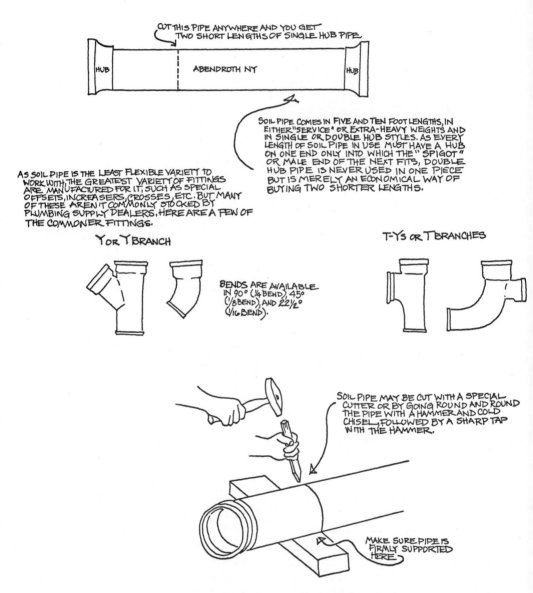

CUT THIS PIPE ANYWHERE AND YOU GET TWO SHORT LENGTHS OF SINGLE HUB PIPE

HUB

ABENDROTH NY

HUB

SOIL PIPE COMES IN FIVE AND TEN FOOT LENGTHS, IN EITHER "SERVICE" OR EXTRA-HEAVY WEIGHTS AND IN SINGLE OR DOUBLE HUB STYLES. AS EVERY LENGTH OF SOIL PIPE IN USE MUST HAVE A HUB ON ONE END ONLY INTO WHICH THE "SPIGOT" OR MALE END OF THE NEXT FITS, DOUBLE HUB PIPE IS NEVER USED IN ONE PIECE BUT IS MERELY AN ECONOMICAL WAY OF BUYING TWO SHORTER LENGTHS.

AS SOIL PIPE IS THE LEAST FLEXIBLE VARIETY TO WORK WITH, THE GREATEST VARIETY OF FITTINGS ARE MANUFACTURED FOR IT, SUCH AS SPECIAL OFFSETS, INCREASERS, CROSSES, ETC. BUT MANY OF THESE AREN'T COMMONLY STOCKED BY PLUMBING SUPPLY DEALERS, HERE ARE A FEW OF THE COMMONER FITTINGS.

Y OR Y BRANCH

T-YS OR T BRANCHES

BENDS ARE AVAILABLE IN 90° (¼ BEND), 45° (⅛ BEND), AND 22½° (⅟₁₆ BEND).

SOIL PIPE MAY BE CUT WITH A SPECIAL CUTTER OR BY GOING ROUND AND ROUND THE PIPE WITH A HAMMER AND COLD CHISEL, FOLLOWED BY A SHARP TAP WITH THE HAMMER.

MAKE SURE PIPE IS FIRMLY SUPPORTED HERE

How to work with cast iron soil pipe

TO JOIN SOIL PIPE

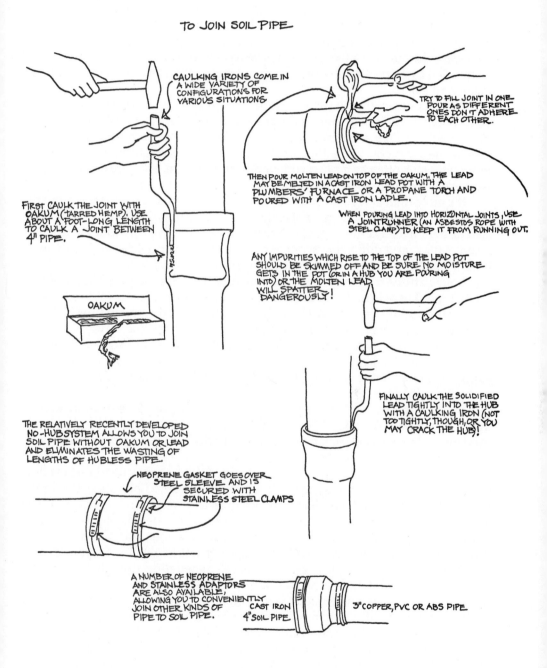

CAULKING IRONS COME IN A WIDE VARIETY OF CONFIGURATIONS FOR VARIOUS SITUATIONS

FIRST CAULK THE JOINT WITH OAKUM (TARRED HEMP). USE ABOUT A FOOT-LONG LENGTH TO CAULK A JOINT BETWEEN 4" PIPE.

OAKUM

TRY TO FILL JOINT IN ONE POUR AS DIFFERENT ONES DON'T ADHERE TO EACH OTHER.

THEN POUR MOLTEN LEAD ON TOP OF THE OAKUM. THE LEAD MAY BE MELTED IN A CAST IRON LEAD POT WITH A PLUMBERS' FURNACE OR A PROPANE TORCH AND POURED WITH A CAST IRON LADLE.

WHEN POURING LEAD INTO HORIZONTAL JOINTS, USE A JOINT RUNNER (AN ASBESTOS ROPE WITH STEEL CLAMP) TO KEEP IT FROM RUNNING OUT.

ANY IMPURITIES WHICH RISE TO THE TOP OF THE LEAD POT SHOULD BE SKIMMED OFF AND BE SURE NO MOISTURE GETS IN THE POT (OR IN A HUB YOU ARE POURING INTO) OR THE MOLTEN LEAD WILL SPATTER DANGEROUSLY!

FINALLY CAULK THE SOLIDIFIED LEAD TIGHTLY INTO THE HUB WITH A CAULKING IRON (NOT TOO TIGHTLY, THOUGH, OR YOU MAY CRACK THE HUB)!

THE RELATIVELY RECENTLY DEVELOPED NO-HUB SYSTEM ALLOWS YOU TO JOIN SOIL PIPE WITHOUT OAKUM OR LEAD AND ELIMINATES THE WASTING OF LENGTHS OF HUBLESS PIPE.

NEOPRENE GASKET GOES OVER STEEL SLEEVE AND IS SECURED WITH STAINLESS STEEL CLAMPS

A NUMBER OF NEOPRENE AND STAINLESS ADAPTORS ARE ALSO AVAILABLE, ALLOWING YOU TO CONVENIENTLY JOIN OTHER KINDS OF PIPE TO SOIL PIPE.

CAST IRON 4" SOIL PIPE

3" COPPER, PVC OR ABS PIPE

maximum safe distance from fixture to vent is 1' per ¼" of the fixture's drain diameter. A tub with customary 1½" drain could thus be up to 6' away from its vent, while a lavatory (1¼") could be but 5' (the New York state code conservatively shrinks these figures to 3½' and 2½' respectively). If a maximum is exceeded, the offending fixture must have its own vent stack or must be revented (connected by a special vent pipe at a point higher than any other fixture) to the main vent stack.

Another rule of thumb (which *will* satisfy most codes) is that the diameter of a vent should never be less than the largest drain diameter of any fixture it services. As a toilet requires a minimum of a 3" drain, a whole bathroom would thus necessitate a 3" vent, while that serving a kitchen sink might be 1½". Although these rules may often be broken with impunity, take care: They are usually treated with great seriousness by plumbing inspectors!

It's more than likely that your old-house waste system is composed primarily of cast iron soil pipe. The great strength and durability of this pipe made it the standard for over a century (it still is required by some codes), but it is extremely heavy, bulky, and difficult to work with. You may nevertheless rejoice if you do have a cast iron system, for it isn't likely to call for attention.

Your fixtures may very likely be joined to the soil pipe by a length of lead waste pipe. There is no harm in having lead here, for it does its job well and its toxicity is certainly irrelevant. The only shortcoming of this waste pipe is that its extreme softness renders it vulnerable to sagging, kinking, and physical violence of any kind. I recently had the misguided accuracy to bore a neat hole through the middle of a hidden lead drain, through which I innocently routed a new copper supply. As I had never felt the bit passing through the lead, it took some time to account for the leak.

DWV (drain-waste-vent) copper tubing became a popular substitute for cast iron during the 1950s and 1960s, but this excellent pipe is unfortunately rarely used today due to its exorbitant price. Its popularity has recently been usurped by the inexpensive ABS (black) and PVC (white) Schedule 40 plastic pipes. (A much lighter grade of PVC is usually sold at do-it-yourself stores. Be sure to get Schedule 40.) These are extremely easy to work with and appear to hold up well over the years (although they haven't had a chance to be truly tested in this respect). The solvent used to join them to their fittings creates a permanent leak-proof "weld," but is unfortunately highly toxic in its liquid and gaseous states. If you use it, breathe as little as possible of its vapors and try not to get any on your skin.

Although it may require great patience, penetrating thought, and dirty, sometimes exasperating labor, old-house plumbing is unexpectedly and richly rewarding. No other involvement with your old-house will give you a greater feeling of intimacy with it than will the performance of a successful operation on its plumbing system. You unfortunately won't be permitted to operate without a license in most cities, but you may very well be able to make the same kind of arrangement with the possessor of a plumber's license as that you made with the electrician.

10

The Digestive and Respiratory Systems: Old-House Energy Consumption and Ventilation

The earliest American homes were heated entirely with wood burned in one or more fireplaces. Although most of us would agree that these are uniquely sensual and soul-satisfying sources of heat, they are voracious consumers of fuel. Their reputation for energy inefficiency has indeed recently fallen to such a low ebb that they have often been accused of being heat *losses* rather than sources. Although this would certainly be true of an unused fireplace without a damper (an iron flap pivoted in the constricted portion or throat of a chimney), it would surely be a slanderous charge against a roaring fire on the hearth. If it were not, how could we account for the warmth of my house one night last winter when my fireplace pinch hit for my energy-efficient furnace, whose oil line froze at twenty below zero?

The notorious inefficiency of the country's first heat source nevertheless led Benjamin Franklin to conceive his Pennsylvania fireplace as early as 1744. This cast iron "Franklin stove" with doors that could be closed or left open was inserted into an existing fireplace to improve its efficiency (anticipating today's multitude of such energy-saving contraptions by more than two hundred years). The first free-standing woodstoves made their appearance around the time of the American Revolution, proving to be the vanguard of a long line of wood- and coal-burning devices (each new model of which was guaranteed to be more attractive and efficient than any of its predecessors) extending right down to the present day.

Despite the continuing association of old-houses with fireplaces and wood-stoves, it would be a mistake to consider central heating systems as recent intrusions. Wood- or coal-fired hot air furnaces have actually been in use since 1800. The heat produced by the fuel burned in the firebox or combustion chamber of such a furnace was transferred to the air filling the plenum, or air chamber, that surrounded it. This hot air was then ducted to the various rooms of the house, while the cooler, heavier air that collected at their bottoms fell back to the furnace through cold air returns. Much the same gravity hot air system is still in use today, although an electric fan or blower is usually added to hurry the hot air on its way, making it a forced hot air system.

Central steam heating systems also made their appearance about the same time, in which water was heated in the water jacket surrounding the combustion chamber of a boiler until it turned to steam, which was then piped to radiators in the various rooms of the house. The simplest of these was the one-pipe gravity

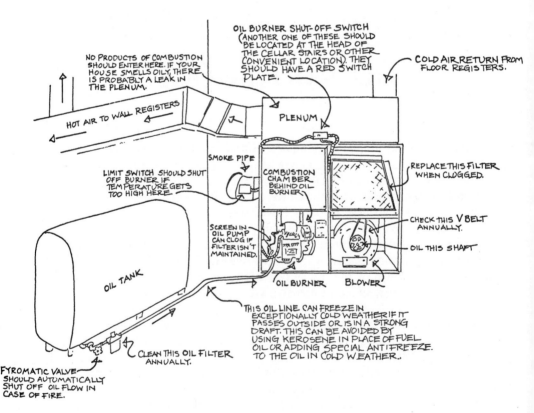

A forced hot air heating system

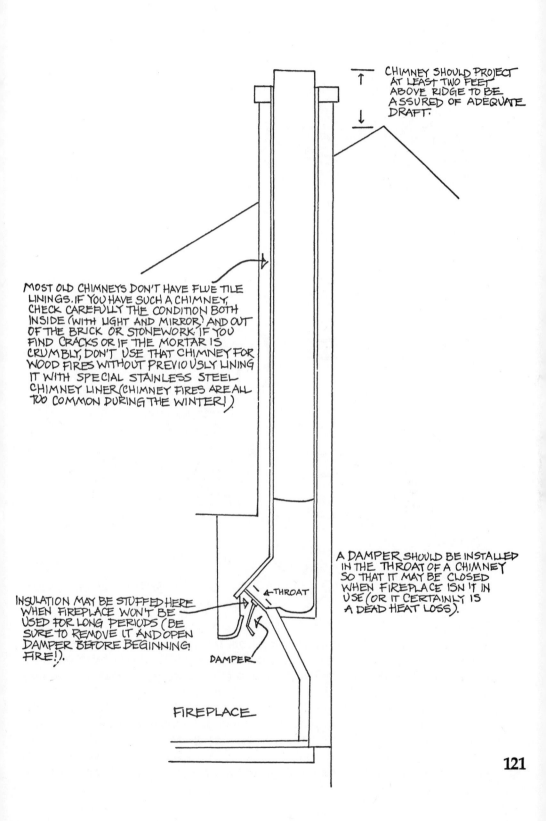

CHIMNEY SHOULD PROJECT AT LEAST TWO FEET ABOVE RIDGE TO BE ASSURED OF ADEQUATE DRAFT.

MOST OLD CHIMNEYS DON'T HAVE FLUE TILE LININGS. IF YOU HAVE SUCH A CHIMNEY, CHECK CAREFULLY THE CONDITION BOTH INSIDE (WITH LIGHT AND MIRROR) AND OUT OF THE BRICK OR STONEWORK. IF YOU FIND CRACKS OR IF THE MORTAR IS CRUMBLY, DON'T USE THAT CHIMNEY FOR WOOD FIRES WITHOUT PREVIOUSLY LINING IT WITH SPECIAL STAINLESS STEEL CHIMNEY LINER (CHIMNEY FIRES ARE ALL TOO COMMON DURING THE WINTER!).

A DAMPER SHOULD BE INSTALLED IN THE THROAT OF A CHIMNEY SO THAT IT MAY BE CLOSED WHEN FIREPLACE ISN'T IN USE (OR IT CERTAINLY IS A DEAD HEAT LOSS).

INSULATION MAY BE STUFFED HERE WHEN FIREPLACE WON'T BE USED FOR LONG PERIODS (BE SURE TO REMOVE IT AND OPEN DAMPER BEFORE BEGINNING FIRE!).

THROAT

DAMPER

FIREPLACE

121

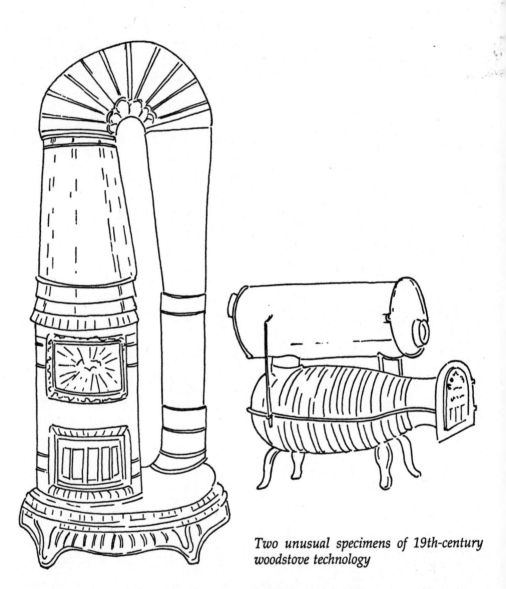

Two unusual specimens of 19th-century woodstove technology

system, in which both the steam rising from the boiler, and the condensate, or water formed as the steam cooled, traveled in opposite directions through the same pipe. This often resulted in a "traffic jam" announced by the familiar rattling and clanking of the radiators when the heat first came on.

The hot water central heating system wasn't introduced into houses until around 1880, but its lower operating temperature and consequent reduction of safety hazards quickly caused it to become more popular than steam heat. The two systems are otherwise quite similar, although a circulation pump is a necessary addition to the newer system in order to force hot water from the boiler to the

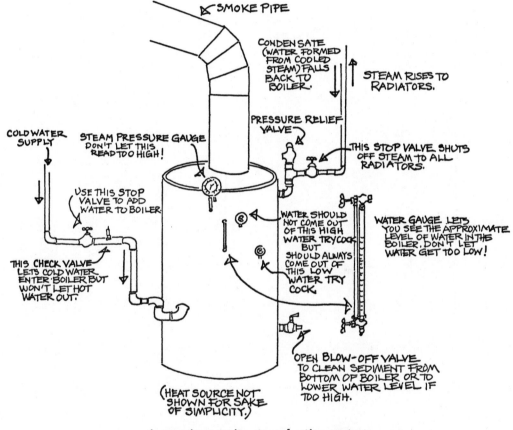

SMOKE PIPE

CONDENSATE (WATER FORMED FROM COOLED STEAM) FALLS BACK TO BOILER.

STEAM RISES TO RADIATORS.

PRESSURE RELIEF VALVE

COLD WATER SUPPLY

STEAM PRESSURE GAUGE. DON'T LET THIS READ TOO HIGH!

THIS STOP VALVE SHUTS OFF STEAM TO ALL RADIATORS.

USE THIS STOP VALVE TO ADD WATER TO BOILER.

WATER SHOULD NOT COME OUT OF THIS HIGH WATER TRY COCK BUT SHOULD ALWAYS COME OUT OF THIS LOW WATER TRY COCK.

WATER GAUGE LETS YOU SEE THE APPROXIMATE LEVEL OF WATER IN THE BOILER. DON'T LET WATER GET TOO LOW!

THIS CHECK VALVE LETS COLD WATER ENTER BOILER BUT WON'T LET HOT WATER OUT.

OPEN BLOW-OFF VALVE TO CLEAN SEDIMENT FROM BOTTOM OF BOILER OR TO LOWER WATER LEVEL IF TOO HIGH.

(HEAT SOURCE NOT SHOWN FOR SAKE OF SIMPLICITY.)

A one-pipe gravity steam heating system

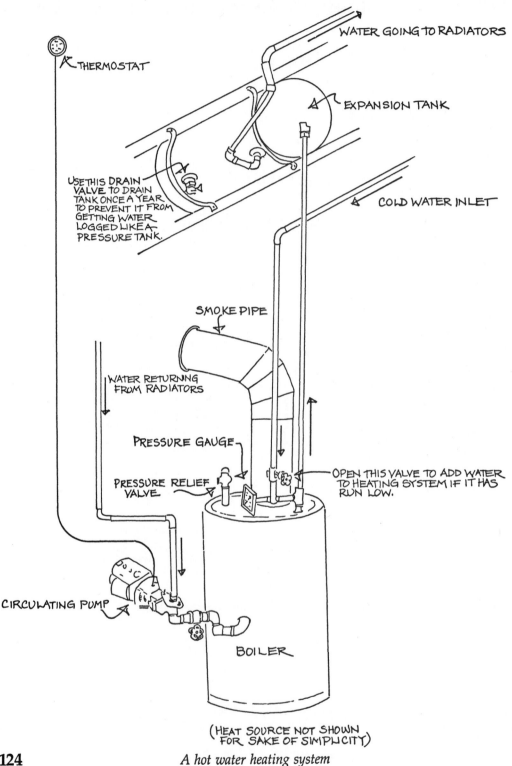

WATER GOING TO RADIATORS

THERMOSTAT

EXPANSION TANK

USE THIS DRAIN VALVE TO DRAIN TANK ONCE A YEAR TO PREVENT IT FROM GETTING WATER LOGGED LIKE A PRESSURE TANK.

COLD WATER INLET

SMOKE PIPE

WATER RETURNING FROM RADIATORS

PRESSURE GAUGE

OPEN THIS VALVE TO ADD WATER TO HEATING SYSTEM IF IT HAS RUN LOW.

PRESSURE RELIEF VALVE

CIRCULATING PUMP

BOILER

(HEAT SOURCE NOT SHOWN FOR SAKE OF SIMPLICITY)

A hot water heating system

radiators or convectors. As the entire system is always filled with water, an expansion tank near the boiler must also be added to a hot water system in order to accommodate the increased volume of water when it's heated.

Whether you have fireplace, woodstove, or central heating system, it's most important to keep them well maintained for maximum safety and fuel economy. Chimneys, smoke pipes, boilers, stoves, radiators, and furnaces should be thoroughly cleaned just before every heating season, as should blowers, air and oil filters, thermostats, and oil burner nozzles and electrodes. The draft, carbon content, and temperature of the exhaust gases of furnaces and boilers should also be measured at this time and from them their operating efficiencies calculated. As the cleaning of chimneys and smoke pipes is undoubtedly the dirtiest of all old-house tasks and the calculating of furnace efficiency requires several expensive instruments, I suggest that you hire professionals for these jobs.*

The inefficiency of the digestive systems of our old-houses has recently been the subject of an enormous amount of unfavorable publicity. We've not only been advised to maintain efficient heating systems, but have been cajoled to curb their voracious appetites for fuel in many other ways: "Save up to 30 percent of your house's energy consumption by installing aluminum storm windows!" "Cut heating costs 20 percent by adding to your attic insulation!" "Caulking and weatherstripping can save you 35 percent of your fuel bill!" If we put our old-houses on every such diet we have had recommended to us, we could then surely retire on the monthly checks we would *receive* from the fuel companies!

The cost of energy today is indeed prodigious, yet is your old-house really such a reprehensible power-gobbler? Recent studies by the Energy Research and Development Administration attribute the worst energy efficiency to houses built between 1940 and 1975. Buildings constructed since that time owe their superior efficiency to being weatherstripped, insulation-stuffed, caulked, and sealed to within an inch of their lives. But what accounts for the similar success of old-houses built prior to World War II?

Old-houses were usually carefully sited for maximum protection from winter winds and summer sun. They were rarely built in exposed locations (no matter how magnificent the view) and were often protected by the thoughtful placement of their barns and other outbuildings between them and the prevailing weather. This practice was perfected by the New England farmer, who often attached his outbuildings to his farmhouse in a long chain. This simultaneously shielded it from winter storms and allowed him to do most of his chores without once going outside.

Deciduous trees were planted to the south of many old-houses, so their summer foliage would filter out the strong sun of that season, while their bare branches wouldn't impede the treasured solar radiation in winter. Evergreen

---

*Chimney sweeps were until very recently as rare as horse-drawn carriages—now they advertise in every paper. Your fuel company will offer a reasonable service contract for your oil burner and furnace.

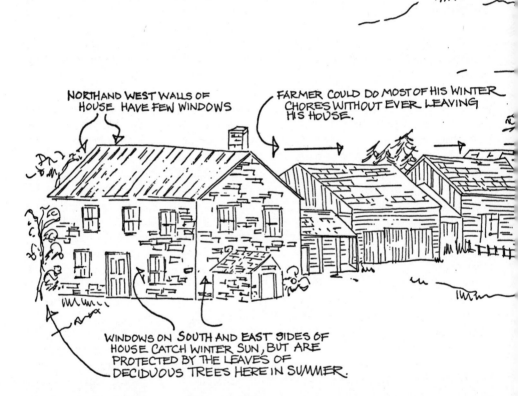

NORTH AND WEST WALLS OF HOUSE HAVE FEW WINDOWS

FARMER COULD DO MOST OF HIS WINTER CHORES WITHOUT EVER LEAVING HIS HOUSE.

WINDOWS ON SOUTH AND EAST SIDES OF HOUSE CATCH WINTER SUN, BUT ARE PROTECTED BY THE LEAVES OF DECIDUOUS TREES HERE IN SUMMER.

windbreaks were also commonly located to the north and west of a house, where they very effectively weakened the force of wintry winds. The U.S. government made its own energy-saving pitch during the Great Depression, claiming that a good windbreak could reduce the fuel consumption of a house by as much as 30 percent (the very same claim made today by the purveyors of aluminum storm windows).

Old-house windows were usually fewer and smaller than those of newer structures and invariably favored southern exposures, thus minimizing heat loss while maximizing solar gain. Shutters, awnings, and porches weren't merely ornamental appendages to a building but served to protect it and its inhabitants from the weather. Entries (now more often referred to by their space-age alias of

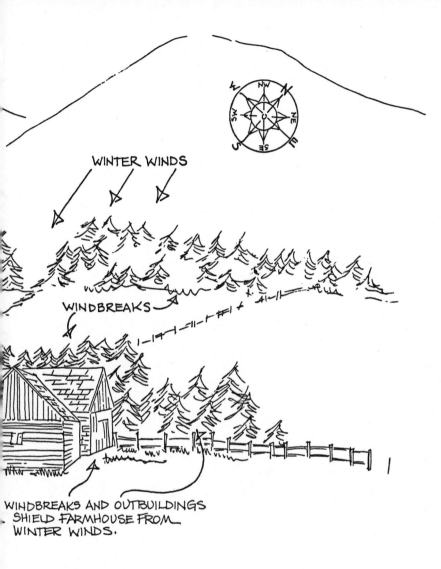

WINTER WINDS

WINDBREAKS

WINDBREAKS AND OUTBUILDINGS
SHIELD FARMHOUSE FROM
WINTER WINDS.

The energy efficiency of a New England farm

"air locks") were extremely effective means of keeping precious warm air from pouring out of a house whenever its outside door was opened.

Yet no matter what energy-saving features a house of any age might have, it's no more efficient than its owner makes it. This surprising fact was dramatically demonstrated by a recent Princeton University study in which the energy-uses of a number of families of the same size living in identical houses in the same town were carefully audited. Some families actually used more than twice as much energy as others during the same period of time.

You should thus be well advised to seriously question your own habits of energy-use before expending time and money on energy-saving improvements or retrofits to your old-house. Lowering the thermostat setting but a few degrees will **127**

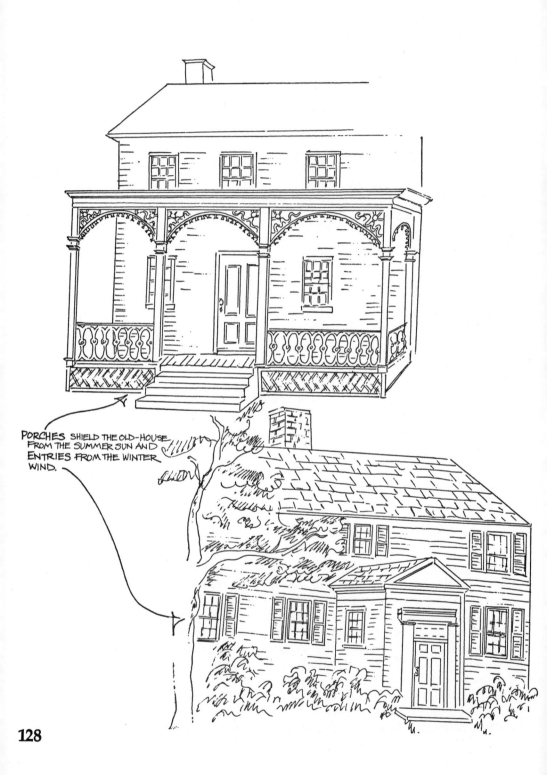

PORCHES SHIELD THE OLD-HOUSE
FROM THE SUMMER SUN AND
ENTRIES FROM THE WINTER
WIND.

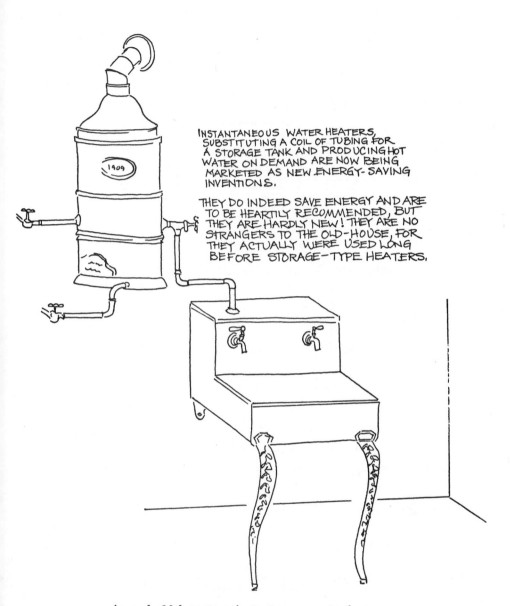

INSTANTANEOUS WATER HEATERS, SUBSTITUTING A COIL OF TUBING FOR A STORAGE TANK AND PRODUCING HOT WATER ON DEMAND ARE NOW BEING MARKETED AS NEW ENERGY- SAVING INVENTIONS.

THEY DO INDEED SAVE ENERGY AND ARE TO BE HEARTILY RECOMMENDED, BUT THEY ARE HARDLY NEW! THEY ARE NO STRANGERS TO THE OLD-HOUSE, FOR THEY ACTUALLY WERE USED LONG BEFORE STORAGE-TYPE HEATERS.

An early-20th-century instantaneous water heater

often decrease the fuel consumption of a furnace or water heater by a seemingly disproportionate amount. Wearing warmer clothes and using more blankets on your bed will easily make up for such a reduction in heat and the air in your house will be better for breathing.

Electric appliances that heat or cool anything, such as water heaters, frost-free refrigerators, freezers, dryers, and air conditioners are extremely expensive to operate—use them with restraint. There is no need to heat all the rooms of your house equally in the winter, for some activities are actually more comfortable at lower temperatures. Cutting off or reducing the flow of heat to nonessential **129**

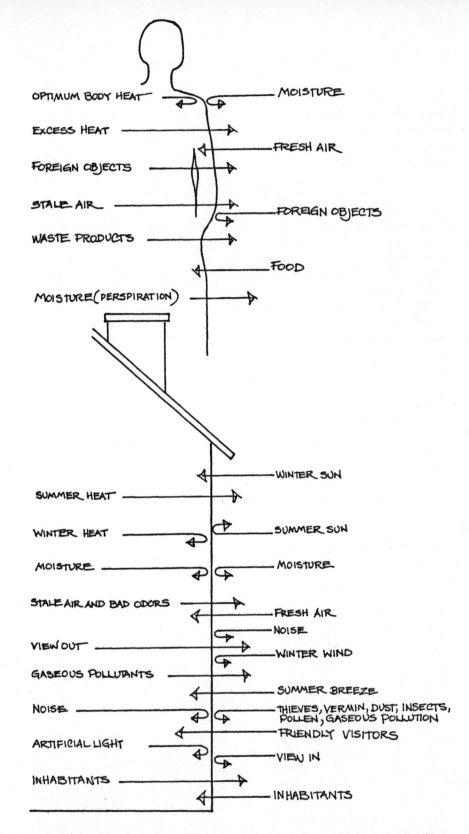

The skins of both the human body and the house must function as highly selective filters

rooms, just as our bodies reduce the flow of blood to our extremities during cold weather, should go a long way toward cutting your energy costs.

When you're satisfied your energy use is as low as it can comfortably be and that you're utilizing the energy-saving capabilities of your old-house to the best advantage, yet your utility bills are still unacceptably high, it's time to retrofit it. I've stressed that this step shouldn't be your first because unlike the energy-saving measures previously considered, retrofitting can be expensive and prove hazardous to the health of your old-house and yourself.

As many retrofitting techniques entail minimizing heat loss by drastically tightening the skin of your house, it's important to understand just how tight it should become. Although most old-houses have far more infiltration of outside air than is required to maintain a healthful environment within, it's possible, although usually extremely difficult, to reduce it to an unhealthful level. All the air in your house should optimally be replaced with fresh air once every hour and a half to two hours. It's more than likely that this rate is being greatly exceeded in your house (there may be several air exchanges every hour). But some super-tight new homes have to wait up to *five* hours for such an exchange!

The inhabitants of these homes have minimal heating bills but may have doomed themselves to breathing air unhealthfully rich in carbon dioxide, carbon monoxide, nitrous oxide, hydrocarbons, and other pollutants. The consciousness of this hazard was very strong a little over one hundred years ago, when the Fresh Air Movement was at its zenith. Lewis Leeds, one of the

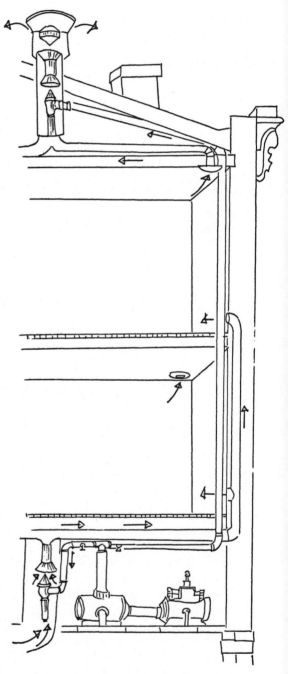

An elaborate 19th-century household ventilating system

131

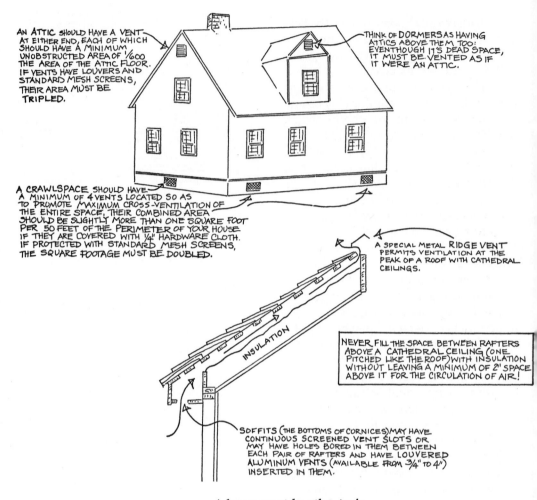

AN ATTIC SHOULD HAVE A VENT AT EITHER END, EACH OF WHICH SHOULD HAVE A MINIMUM UNOBSTRUCTED AREA OF 1/600 THE AREA OF THE ATTIC FLOOR. IF VENTS HAVE LOUVERS AND STANDARD MESH SCREENS, THEIR AREA MUST BE TRIPLED.

THINK OF DORMERS AS HAVING ATTICS ABOVE THEM TOO: EVEN THOUGH IT'S DEAD SPACE, IT MUST BE VENTED AS IF IT WERE AN ATTIC.

A CRAWLSPACE SHOULD HAVE A MINIMUM OF 4 VENTS LOCATED SO AS TO PROMOTE MAXIMUM CROSS-VENTILATION OF THE ENTIRE SPACE. THEIR COMBINED AREA SHOULD BE SLIGHTLY MORE THAN ONE SQUARE FOOT PER 50 FEET OF THE PERIMETER OF YOUR HOUSE IF THEY ARE COVERED WITH 1/4" HARDWARE CLOTH. IF PROTECTED WITH STANDARD MESH SCREENS, THE SQUARE FOOTAGE MUST BE DOUBLED.

A SPECIAL METAL RIDGE VENT PERMITS VENTILATION AT THE PEAK OF A ROOF WITH CATHEDRAL CEILINGS.

INSULATION

NEVER FILL THE SPACE BETWEEN RAFTERS ABOVE A CATHEDRAL CEILING (ONE PITCHED LIKE THE ROOF) WITH INSULATION WITHOUT LEAVING A MINIMUM OF 2' SPACE ABOVE IT FOR THE CIRCULATION OF AIR!

SOFFITS (THE BOTTOMS OF CORNICES) MAY HAVE CONTINUOUS SCREENED VENT SLOTS OR MAY HAVE HOLES BORED IN THEM BETWEEN EACH PAIR OF RAFTERS AND HAVE LOUVERED ALUMINUM VENTS (AVAILABLE FROM 3/4" TO 4") INSERTED IN THEM.

A house must breathe, too!

movement's spokesmen, claimed that the "spent breath" (rich in carbon dioxide) of the occupants of poorly ventilated homes accounted for 40 percent of all deaths in the country. Harriet Beecher Stowe went even further than Leeds, asserting in 1869 that more than *half* the nation were "starved and poisoned" by "tight sleeping-rooms and air-tight stoves!"

A. J. Downing, Dr. Arnott, Leeds, Stowe, and others followed up their dire statistics with a vigorous campaign to introduce fresh air into stagnant American homes, designing ingenious and complicated ventilating systems to accomplish this end. Yet a century later many of us are sleeping in tighter rooms heated with tighter stoves than the fresh air advocates could ever have imagined, having evidently forgotten the importance of breathing in our concern to conserve energy.

As important as good ventilation is for our own well-being, it's if anything even more crucial for that of our houses. The free movement of air in the attic, walls, cellar, and crawlspace of an old-house is necessary to evaporate and diffuse the moisture that may collect there. Without ventilation, this would quickly saturate wooden portions of the structure, providing an ideal environment for wood-destroying fungi.

Some of this moisture may occur as a result of leaks in the roof, siding, cellar walls, or plumbing system of your old-house, but even if there are no such imperfections, it will inevitably occur as the result of the condensation of water vapor in the air. This occurs due to the propensity of warm air to hold more vapor than cold. When it's cooled to the point at which it can no longer hold all its moisture, it has reached its dewpoint and droplets of water will spontaneously form on surrounding surfaces.

You could successfully argue that no such condensation would occur if you could sufficiently lower the vapor content of the air in your house. Some energy conservationists indeed advise us to give up our morning showers, stop boiling water for coffee or potatoes, and throw away our potted plants in order to accomplish this! The fallacy in this approach is that a minimum vapor content of 30 to 35 percent *must* be maintained to preserve the good health of ourselves and our old-houses, for a dangerous drying out of both old wood and mucous membranes occurs at lesser concentrations.

Dewpoint, condensation, and vapor barriers

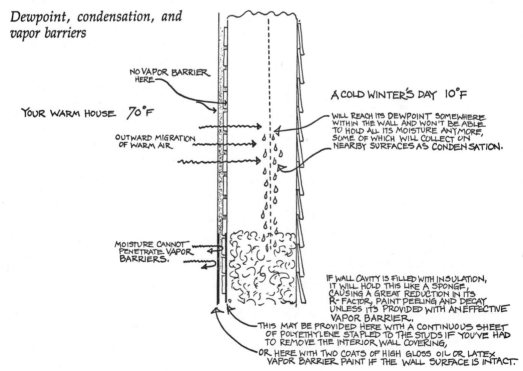

NO VAPOR BARRIER HERE

YOUR WARM HOUSE 70°F

OUTWARD MIGRATION OF WARM AIR

MOISTURE CANNOT PENETRATE VAPOR BARRIERS.

A COLD WINTER'S DAY 10°F

WILL REACH ITS DEWPOINT SOMEWHERE WITHIN THE WALL AND WON'T BE ABLE TO HOLD ALL ITS MOISTURE ANYMORE, SOME OF WHICH WILL COLLECT ON NEARBY SURFACES AS CONDENSATION.

IF WALL CAVITY IS FILLED WITH INSULATION, IT WILL HOLD THIS LIKE A SPONGE, CAUSING A GREAT REDUCTION IN ITS R-FACTOR, PAINT PEELING AND DECAY UNLESS IT'S PROVIDED WITH AN EFFECTIVE VAPOR BARRIER.

THIS MAY BE PROVIDED HERE WITH A CONTINUOUS SHEET OF POLYETHYLENE STAPLED TO THE STUDS IF YOU'VE HAD TO REMOVE THE INTERIOR WALL COVERING,

OR HERE WITH TWO COATS OF HIGH GLOSS OIL OR LATEX VAPOR BARRIER PAINT IF THE WALL SURFACE IS INTACT.

Unless the atmosphere in your house is unusually humid, a far more reasonable approach to coping with water vapor is to control *where* it will condense through the use of vapor barriers. If you have had the misfortune to have been forced to strip the inner wall and ceiling surfaces from your old-house, you may staple a continuous sheet of 6 mil (.006″ thick) polyethylene to studs and joists before you apply new wall and ceiling surfaces. If your old-house has a crawlspace over moist earth, lay another sheet of plastic here, weighted down with rocks, to keep moisture from evaporating into the air, later to condense on joists and subfloor. Such impermeable barriers will prevent vapor from migrating into the wall and attic spaces of your house, where it would condense and lead to decay if these areas weren't sufficiently ventilated.

As an enormous amount of vapor is funneled through even the smallest chink in such armor, you must apply it with meticulous care. Try not to puncture or tear the plastic (seal it with tape if you do) and fit it tightly around doors, windows, and electrical outlets (these should be further protected with special foam gaskets that may be purchased to fit under their cover plates). If you were able to leave the plastered or paneled walls and ceilings of your old-house intact, you may still provide them with effective vapor barriers by sealing them with two coats of high-gloss oil or latex vapor barrier paint, which may be subsequently covered with a paint of your choice.

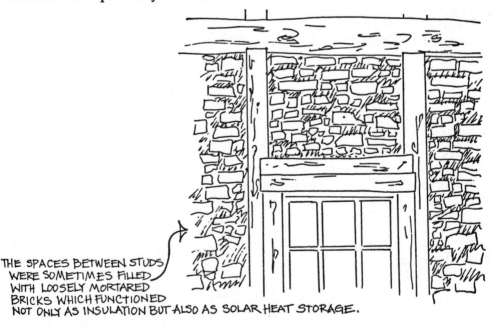

THE SPACES BETWEEN STUDS WERE SOMETIMES FILLED WITH LOOSELY MORTARED BRICKS WHICH FUNCTIONED NOT ONLY AS INSULATION BUT ALSO AS SOLAR HEAT STORAGE.

THE SUBSTANTIAL AMOUNT OF HEAT PICKED UP DURING A SUNNY DAY AND RADIATED AT NIGHT IS UNPLEASANT IN SUMMER, BUT MORE THAN WELCOME IN WINTER.

Early insulation

If you succeeded in creating a tight vapor barrier, you will also have gone a long way toward eliminating the single greatest heat loss in your house. This is the infiltration of cold outside air through cracks and holes in the structure's skin. It has been estimated that the combined area of every such hole and crack in an average old-house would be equivalent to an *open window* 3' wide by 5' high! Visit every room of your house on a very cold day, passing the back of your hand in front of every suspicious opening in floor, ceiling, and exterior wall and you'll probably feel enough infiltration to make you "see" that window. It shouldn't take much more persuasion to send you off to a hardware or building supply dealer to buy an assortment of the multitudinous caulking and weatherstripping products now available to seal all those holes and cracks.

The next most important and by far the most widely publicized retrofit to an old-house is the insulation of its skin to help retain heat. This isn't a concept that entirely escaped the attention of our forefathers, for old-houses were frequently insulated with a variety of materials. Spaces between studs were often filled with loosely mortared bricks, while both walls and ceilings were insulated with newspapers, seaweed, wood shavings, corn cobs, sawdust, or "Dutch biscuits" (cakes of mud and straw), depending on the age and locality of the house. The chief disadvantage of any of these materials is that they aren't nearly as good insulators as the substances recently developed specifically for the purpose, although these may pose additional problems of their own (see Table 2).

Every material has a specific thermal conductivity or rate at which it will transfer heat to an adjoining surface. This rate is also known as a material's K-factor and represents the number of BTUs (British Thermal Units—one BTU is

Table 2: Thermal Properties of Common Building Materials[1]

One Square Foot of Material One Inch Thick[4]	Thermal Conductivity[2] or K-factor	Thermal Resistance[3] or R-factor	Characteristics
Polyisocyanurate Foam	.14	7.20	Thermax, Hi-R, Yellowish, comes in 4'×8' sheets with foil facing on both sides. Recent, expensive product. Toxicity not yet established.
Polyurethane Foam	.16	6.25	Yellowish, contains refrigerant gas instead of air in foam bubbles. Comes in unfaced 4'×8' sheets. Releases toxic gases when burning.
Still Air	.17	5.88	This is the secret to the success of most insulating materials: their R value rises in proportion to their capacity to entrap it.

One Square Foot of Material One Inch Thick[4]	Thermal Conductivity[2] or K-factor	Thermal Resistance[3] or R-factor	Characteristics
Extruded Polystyrene Foam	.18	5.41	Styrofoam. Usually blue. Comes in 2'×8' sheets, water resistant. Releases toxic gases when burning.
Expanded Polystyrene Foam	.24	4.17	Often called beadboard. Durovon. Comes in white 2'×8' sheets, water degradable. Releases toxic gases when burning.
Urea-Formaldehyde Foam	.24	4.16	Foamed directly into wall cavities. Releases toxic quantities of formaldehyde gas when heated to but 97°F. (It was banned nationwide, but the ban was overturned by a court order in April 1983.)
Cellulose	.29	3.45	Loose fill, blown or poured in cavities. Highly inflammable shredded newspaper, unless treated with large amounts of boric acid, which may corrode wires or cause allergic reactions.
Rock Wool	.29	3.45	Comes in rolls or batts, but has been largely superseded by fiber glass. Very fine particles extremely irritating to skin and lungs. Fireproof except for paper backing and binder.
Fiber Glass Batts or Rolls[5]	.32	3.16	Fiberglas. Comes in rolls or batts, nontoxic. Fine air-borne particles irritating to skin, throat, and lungs. Rodents love it for nests. Fireproof except for paper backing and binder.
Perlite	.34	2.94	Loose fill, poured in cavities (also used as lightweight aggregate in gypsum plaster). Nontoxic, fireproof natural volcanic glass. Fine particles could lung disease.
Impregnated Fiber Board	.35	2.86	Celotex. Comes in 4'×8' sheets, used for sheathing or interior wall surface. Nontoxic but inflammable.

One Square Foot of Material One Inch Thick[4]	Thermal Conductivity[2] or K-factor	Thermal Resistance[3] or R-factor	Characteristics
Vermiculite	.37	2.70	Loose fill, poured in cavities (also used as synthetic soil). Fireproof, mica-rich silicate rock. As it commonly contains asbestos, it could cause lung cancer.
Sawdust	.41	2.44	Once used extensively as insulation. Hygroscopic (absorbs moisture easily) and inflammable.
White Pine	.78	1.28	Sheathing, siding or paneling. Denser, harder woods have lower R factors. Nontoxic, inflammable.
Common Brick or Gypsum Plaster	5.00	0.20	Brick, see stone. Cement plaster has lower R-factor, but the addition of horse hair in early plasters may compensate for this.
Glass	8.28	0.12	Considering the extreme thinness of a pane of glass, windows obviously have incredibly low R-factors, unless double-glazed with layer of still air between.
Stone or Concrete	10.00	0.10	Extremely low R-factor partially compensated for by high thermal inertia (M-factor) which lengthens the time required to transmit heat.
Aluminum	1421.00	0.0007	Incredibly low R-factor questions its suitability for use in storm doors and windows and as siding for practical (as well as aesthetic) considerations.

[1]As K and R factors vary considerably with density and temperature, the values given are only approximate.

[2]In BTU's per hour per square foot at 1°F temperature differential.

[3]R-factor $= \dfrac{1}{\text{K-factor}}$

[4]To obtain approximate R value of a greater thickness of material, simply multiply by total thickness in inches.

[5]If used as loose fill, R-factor drops to 2.30.

Table 3

Every customer of a utility company in the country is entitled to a *free* computer-assisted energy audit to determine the feasibility of various retrofits to their house. Just call your utility company to arrange for this valuable service, mandated by the federal government and paid for by a surcharge added to the utility's rates (this means that you're paying for the audit whether or not you take advantage of it).

PARAGON POWER CORP. RESIDENTIAL ENERGY AUDIT*

Procedure	Recommendation	Annual Savings	Contracted Cost	Contracted Payback	Do-It-Yourself Cost	Do-It-Yourself Payback
Insulate attic	Insulate with six inches of fiber glass	$143	$450	3.1 Yrs.	$200	1.4 Yrs.
Insulate floor	Not applicable	——	——	——	——	
Insulate exterior walls	Insulate with four inches of blown cellulose	$32	$425	13.3	Not applicable	
Storm doors and windows	Adequate	——	——	——	——	
Caulk and weatherstrip doors & windows	4 Doors 22 windows	$114	$375	3.3	$103	.9
Insulate water heater	Insulate with six inches of fiber glass	$32	$26	.8	$15	.5
Install solar water heater	Install solar water heater & three 21 ft. collectors	$62	$3200	52.0	Not applicable	

*This is a facsimile of part of such an audit; the figures don't necessarily represent actual values.

the amount of heat required to raise the temperature of one pound of water at its maximum density one degree Fahrenheit) per hour that one square foot of it transfers to an adjoining surface which is one degree Fahrenheit warmer or colder than itself. Although a material's K-factor is its basic physical constant, insulation is rated by its thermal resistance or R-factor, which is the reciprocal of its K-factor ($1/K$). As is apparent in Table 2, a system's R-factor thus steadily *increases* as its K-factor *decreases*.

If you want to determine the total thermal performance of a wall, ceiling, or floor composed of several different materials, simply add the K-factors of each material included, multiplying the value given in Table 2 by the number of inches of thickness of each material. The resultant sum represents the total thermal conductivity of a one square foot cross section of a wall, ceiling, or floor and is known as its U-factor. (Its total thermal resistance would be the reciprocal of this.)

If the U-factors of the walls, ceilings, and floors of your old-house seem to you to be too high and you are contemplating insulating them, first take advantage of the *free* computer-assisted energy audit sponsored by your utility company (under federal mandate) in order to see if it would be cost effective to do so. A representative of a private firm hired by the utility will call at your house and gather data which will be relayed to a computer. The resulting energy audit will tell you how many years it would take to break even on each energy-saving measure proposed. In the Paragon Power Corp. audit (see Table 3) it's obvious that it would make excellent sense to insulate your present water heater as you would be reimbursed for your investment in less than a year, but that it wouldn't be cost effective to install a solar hot water heater as it would take fifty-two years to pay for itself!

If you do insulate your house, be extremely careful to provide really tight vapor barriers on the winter-heated side of the insulation. This is of critical importance due to its unfortunate capacity to simultaneously eliminate ventilation and to absorb and retain moisture that may condense in it, often resulting in an optimal environment for fungi. Don't rely on the aluminum foil or Kraft paper backings on some types of insulation to provide such barriers, for it's impossible to join them tightly enough to each other to effectively eliminate the outward migration of moisture. You must therefore never neglect to cover insulation with either the continuous polyethylene or paint film vapor barrier previously mentioned.

Another most important retrofit to an old-house can be the addition of storm doors and windows if it's without them. Although this may be quite expensive, the resultant increase in comfort and decrease in energy costs usually makes it well worth while (a glance at the R-factor of glass in Table 2 will make this obvious). I urge you to resist the importunities of aluminum storm window salespersons, however, for although these may appear financially attractive, they do much to detract from the appearance of an old-house. If aesthetic considerations aren't enough to dissuade you, compare the R-values of wood and aluminum in Table 2.

An energy audit may also reveal that other retrofits could be in order for your old-house. It may recommend that you add new controls to your heating system or change fuels or perhaps install an entirely new system. You may live in an area of the country where solar energy is cost effective. Old-houses are in some ways well adapted to solar conversions, often having southern exposures with steeply pitched roofs ideal for solar collectors and cellars perfect for solar storage. The discussion of such conversions is the subject for a book in itself. However, I can do no more here than refer you to two such volumes (Carter, Strickler) listed in the Bibliography.

Old-House Cosmetics and Ornamentation: Adding and Subtracting Wallpaper, Paint, and Other Adornments

The first American houses were quite naked and unadorned: their bare skin was visible to passersby, while their inhabitants lived in close proximity to the exposed bones of their skeletons. The colonists didn't cause this to be so out of choice, but rather from necessity. Wallpaper, paint, fine hardware, and architectural embellishment were all largely imported from Europe in those days and were consequently scarce and costly. This situation had greatly changed by 1725, when it had become common practice in the more prosperous areas of the country to at least paint both the inside and outside of one's home.

The first preparation used to brighten the interiors of American houses wasn't actually a paint at all, but the well-known thickish solution of slaked lime and water called whitewash. (Slaked lime is calcium hydroxide formed by the chemical combination of lime and water.) Whitewash was at first applied directly to the inside of a building's frame and siding and subsequently to plaster walls and ceilings as they were constructed. This explains why it's so common to discover, upon removing the lath and plaster from the wall of an old-house, the curious fact that someone had apparently painted the inside of the wall.

The first actual paints used on old-house interiors had either linseed oil or water bases, these latter then being known as distemper paints. It wasn't until shortly after 1800 that casein or milk-based paints were introduced into this country from France. The buttermilk or skim-milk paints that are often thought of as being contemporaneous with the colonial period were thus completely unknown at that time.

Calcimine, a preparation of glue, whiting (finely ground limestone powder), and water became a favorite finish for plaster walls and ceilings during the 19th century. The presence of calcimine is often detected (much to the consternation of the old-house painter) by the total inability of a newly applied paint film to adhere to an apparently clean and well-prepared surface. This painter's nightmare may be averted by scrubbing the calcimined surface thoroughly with a solution of warm water and ammonia or washing soda before repainting it.

The evolution of paints used on the exteriors of American houses has been comparatively simple. Linseed oil-based paints have been the unchallenged favorites for this use from early colonial times right up to the middle of the 20th century. Exterior latex water-based paint was developed about that time and has recently attained great popularity. It's an excellent paint, but I can't help feeling that the 250-year alliance of American homes and oil paint makes it a more suitable choice for the old-house.

There has long been much dissension among restorationists as to the colors early American houses were painted. It has become increasingly clear that a wide variety of colors have been popular since very early times, including ivory white, cream, yellow ochre, gray, green, red, and blue. It's more difficult to be sure of the exact shades of these colors, however, as few original formulas for paint manufacture are still in existence and as the colors of painted woodwork or plaster have changed significantly over the course of more than two centuries.

As no one is thus really sure just what early American colors looked like when they were applied, you have considerable latitude in choosing authentic paints for your old-house. It will nonetheless not suffice to select just any shade of the previously mentioned colors, for it might turn out to be more suitable for painting a fire engine or swimming pool than an old-house. What then should be our guidelines in making this important choice?

You must first of all familiarize yourself with authentic shades of color as they appear on wood and plaster (not on paper). You probably need only to analyze the layers of paint that have accumulated on various surfaces in your house in order to accomplish this. The professionals use a surgeon's scalpel and jeweler's glass to do this, but you may utilize a very sharp knife and magnifying glass to good effect. Such analysis will not only give you a complete history of every shade of paint ever used on your house, but may also be interpreted so as to greatly aid in verifying its birth date.

If you can't find a paint that matches one of your old-house's original colors, purchase the smallest can of top-quality oil paint whose color chip proclaims it to be close to your selected shade. Apply a small amount of this to an inconspicuous portion of the part of your house you're painting and let it dry thoroughly. If the resultant shade isn't anything like the original (which it very likely won't be), buy a number of tubes of painter's pigments called colorants, including lampblack,

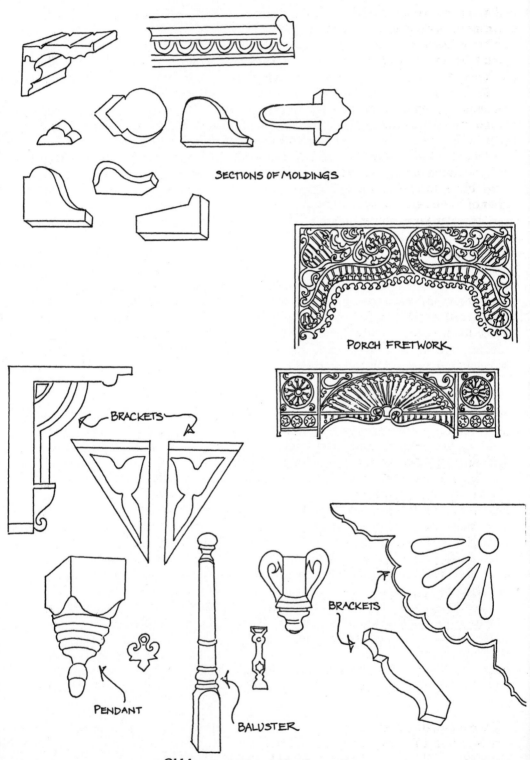

SECTIONS OF MOLDINGS

PORCH FRETWORK

BRACKETS

BRACKETS

PENDANT

BALUSTER

Old-house ornamentation in wood

yellow ochre, venetian red, prussian blue, and burnt sienna. Most premixed colors aren't as dark as early shades, so add a little lampblack first if you don't have any better ideas of your own. Even if you don't fancy yourself an artist, you should be able to alter the shade of a premixed paint to match one of your old-house's colors in a relatively short time.

If your house was built after 1850, you will be more likely to find the shades you require premixed, as paint manufacturers have recently responded to the great demand for authentic Victorian colors. Light, yet not bright shades such as fawn (light reddish brown), gray, and cream were the rule during the third quarter of the 19th century. Darker and more somber colors came into vogue after 1875, including olive green, brick red, brown, deep sage, and dark terra-cotta. It's invariably a mistake to incorporate white in the color scheme of a house from either of these periods, no matter how appropriate it might be for earlier homes.

The later your house may have been built in the 19th century, the more ornamentation it's likely to have been blessed with. The architectural embellishment of gables, cornices, and porches with all manner of turned and jig-sawed wooden finery reached its peak during the Queen Anne period in the 1890s. A severe reaction to the opulence of this architectural style set in around the turn of the century, in which all vestiges of ornamentation were eliminated from the buildings of that day. This reaction was indeed so strong that it persisted during the entire first half of the 20th century, when innumerable stately Victorian

The profuse ornamentation of these two exceptional 19th-century cast iron steam radiators adds to their efficiency as well as their beauty by increasing the area of their radiating surfaces.

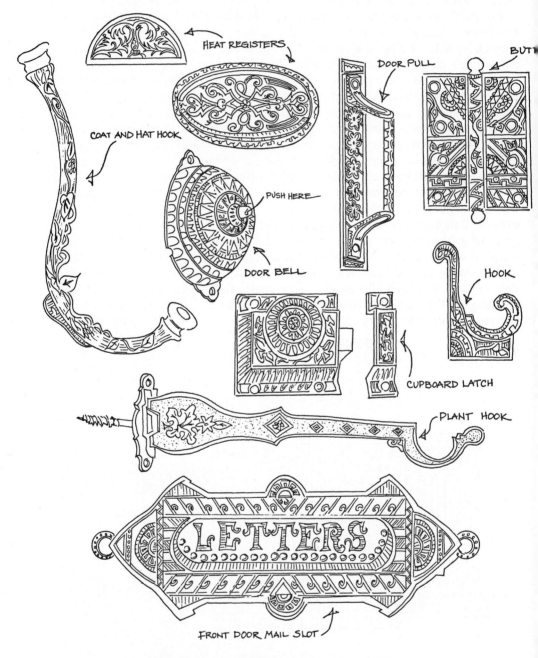

HEAT REGISTERS

BUTT

DOOR PULL

COAT AND HAT HOOK

PUSH HERE

DOOR BELL

HOOK

CUPBOARD LATCH

PLANT HOOK

LETTERS

FRONT DOOR MAIL SLOT

Old-house ornamentation in cast iron and brass

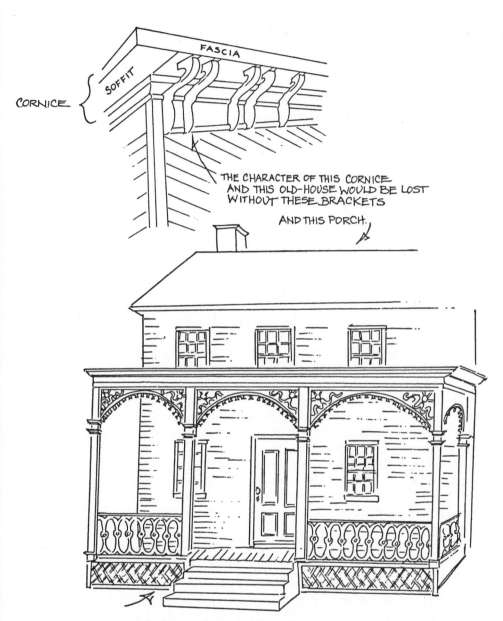

CORNICE

SOFFIT

FASCIA

THE CHARACTER OF THIS CORNICE
AND THIS OLD-HOUSE WOULD BE LOST
WITHOUT THESE BRACKETS

AND THIS PORCH.

houses were either callously stripped of their finery or wantonly torn down and discarded as so much trash.

If your old-house survived this architectural revolution with its full complement of ornamentation, you should give it the long overdue respect it deserves. Always resist the impulse to tear off a porch or simplify a cornice due to their poor condition. Their retention and repair will be well worth the additional effort and expense incurred. Not only should such embellishment be preserved, but it should be emphasized by painting it with colors that contrast with that used on the main body of the house. It was customary during the last half of the 19th **145**

Table 4: Old-House Skin Diseases

Wrinkling and Sagging is caused by applying paint too thickly. The top skin dries out and forms an impenetrable barrier to the drying of the inner portion of the paint film.

Blistering is caused by the building up of fluid pressure underneath the paint, due to rain-soaking or condensation in the wall.

Peeling, Cracking, Flaking, and Scaling are caused by an uncorrected blister situation, resin from knots not previously treated with shellac, wax, or grease on the surface when it was painted—or by painting over a hard, glossy surface.

Alligatoring and Checking are caused by painting over a greasy or oily surface, applying the finish coat during too low a temperature, using a primer with too much oil in it, or not allowing the primer to dry thoroughly.

Bleeding is the emergence of knots and stains through the paint film and is caused by the dissolving of the paint by the resin in knot or stain. It may be avoided by previously applying shellac or a shellac-based primer such as BIN (a proprietary product) to all knots and stains before painting over them.

century to use at least *two* such contrasting colors for trim and ornamentation, resulting in a highly pleasing richness of expression.

Once you've selected a color scheme and obtained the paint to execute it, by far the greatest problem you will usually encounter in painting your old-house is the preparation of the surfaces to be painted. This will probably represent over half the labor you will expend on the paint job if you do it properly (and if you don't, you will have to do it all over again sooner than you might think). The actual painting of the prepared surface may be considered the reward you get for your patient and painstaking preparation.

The magnitude of this preparation is immeasurably increased if you insist on stripping all of the cosmetic accretions of the years from your house in order to reveal the beauty of the unadorned wood beneath. Although I find unfinished or oiled old wood very attractive, I can't make it too clear that complete stripping is rarely a wise procedure:

1. It's almost always extremely time consuming and expensive.

2. It usually *decreases* the authenticity of your old-house, which was probably intended to be painted (unless it was built prior to 1725).

3. It may be hazardous to the health of both your old-house and yourself, depending on the stripping methods you employ.

Even if you are perfectly justified by historical precedent in stripping surfaces (such as removing the layers of paint that may have accumulated on the originally varnished interior woodwork of your late 19th century house), it's highly unlikely you will have any idea of the magnitude of the project. It's an excellent idea for this reason to begin the job by stripping a test area in the most inconspicuous,

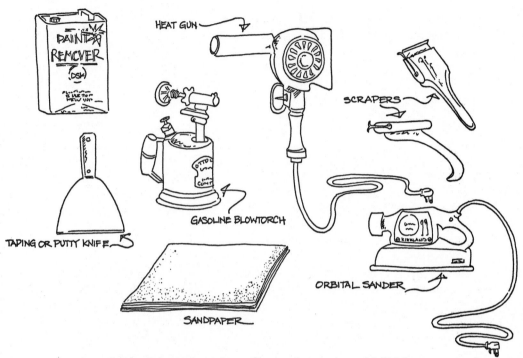

Some of the tools and supplies used to remove old finishes

inaccessible, and complicatedly-contoured location you can find. If your work progresses to your satisfaction there, you will have some assurance that you'll be able to complete the project. If the work is agonizingly slow or the result unsatisfactory, you may abandon the job, touch up the damage, and no one will be the wiser (except yourself, of course).

The methods for stripping or preparing surfaces for painting are numerous and it's extremely important to choose the right one for the particular project. Scraping is undoubtedly the simplest, safest, and cheapest method of removing old finishes, but unfortunately isn't always the fastest. It's particularly useful in preparing exterior surfaces for painting, provided that you keep the blade of your scraper honed to a fine edge with a file. Scrapers with interchangeable triangular and curved blades known as shave hooks can also be extremely useful in removing finishes from corners and the molded surfaces of interior woodwork.

A special rotary disk sander is made for removing paint from clapboards and other siding if a scraper will not suffice. However, such sanding creates dust that may remain airborne for many hours. This may be extremely toxic and is so mobile that it's actually *against the law* in some localities to sand paint off the exterior of your old-house! Sanding is moreover rarely a good method for the removal of paint from interior surfaces, for it likewise may generate enormous quantities of possibly toxic dust and irrevocably destroy the patina, or beautiful surface quality, that wood acquires with age. Although very early floors should be scraped rather than sanded for this reason, floors of no great antiquity may be far more efficiently sanded. Always rent a commercial floor sander and edger for this purpose, for anything else is inadequate. If the floor to be sanded is painted, be sure to request that 80 percent of the paper supplied with the sander is open coat and of the coarsest grit, as this will take longer to get clogged with paint.

The most popular method of stripping wood is probably the utilization of chemical paint removers. It's undeniably satisfying to watch paint films shrivel under their attack, yet the work rarely progresses as quickly as it promises, for you will probably have to apply remover several times to the same spot to ensure the removal of all layers of paint from it. Such chemical preparations are also expensive and more importantly pose a serious threat to your health. Be sure to wear heavy-duty rubber gloves if you do use them, and breathe as little of their vapors as possible.

Removing paint with a gasoline blowtorch, propane torch, or electric paint burner is also a very popular and fairly fast stripping technique, although the use of any of these is dangerous, for they have caused many fires and the fumes released by burning paint can be very toxic. This is notoriously the case when one or more paint layers contain the lead compounds so common to old-house paints. Furthermore, it's almost impossible to remove paint with intense heat without burning or scorching the surface of the wood you are going to so much trouble to reveal.

New products are constantly appearing on the market that claim to make stripping easier and safer than ever before. One of the most likely of these is an electric heat-gun, which resembles a heavy-duty hairdryer. Its merchandisers claim it has none of the above hazards, due to its significantly lower operating temperature. Another likely product combines a chemical paste with a fiber blanket, which combination is purported to remove fourteen layers of paint at once! At relatively little cost, you can rent a new device that greatly speeds the process of chipping loose paint off the exterior of your house by utilizing a high-speed stream of water. This must be handled with great care, however, for it's quite capable of breaking window panes or gouging grooves in your siding.

It's quite likely that some part of the interior of your old-house has received a decorative treatment other than a simple paint job. Wallpaper came into use in this country as early as 1740; but it was imported and consequently scarce and costly, and only affordable by wealthy urban dwellers. This early paper was undoubtedly worth what it cost, for it was handmade and virtually an art form in itself. Wallpaper was rolled and printed by machine in the United States after 1837 and was thereafter far cheaper and easier to acquire throughout the land by those of lesser affluence.

It thus transpired that a vast number of the country cousins of those lucky few who had acquired imported papered parlors pined after their lack of such artistically decorated walls. Completely knowledgeable of their envy, itinerant house decorators hurried from country house to country house, adorning their walls

Two examples of early wallpaper

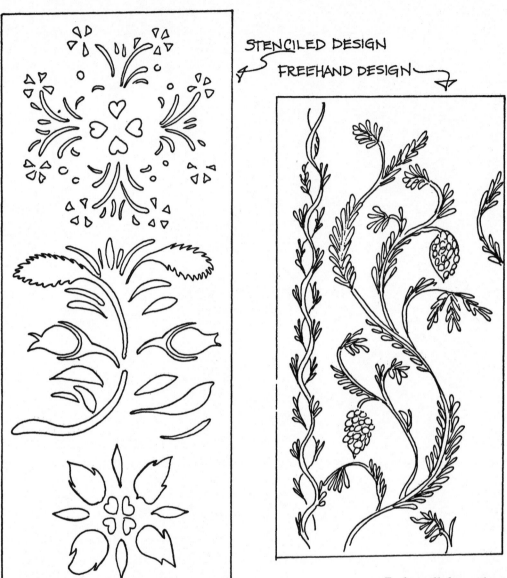

Early wall decorations

with stenciled or freehand designs. Perhaps the country cousins got the better of the bargain after all, for these craftsmen were at times artists of no mean skill and created murals in the American primitive style of great beauty (usually on hall and parlor walls and in particular over the mantel of the parlor fireplace).

These artisans also frequently embellished the woodwork and flooring of these rooms. Floors were customarily painted and stenciled, while woodwork was often meticulously grained or marbleized in imitation of cedar, oak, walnut, or marble. Covering one species of wood (almost always pine) with paint so applied as to make it look like another species or material may seem artificial and undesirable. Yet it was sometimes executed with such consummate artistry that **150** it's impossible not to admire it.

MURAL

As you may have one or more of these decorative treatments under subsequent layers of paint or wallpaper in your old-house, great care should be taken not to damage them when removing overlying material. If you suspect their presence, don't use heat or abrasives to strip the paint that may conceal them, but rather carefully remove one layer at a time with a chemical remover. Wallpaper may be safely removed with an easily rentable wallpaper steamer or a homemade equivalent utilizing a garden hose and a steam radiator. I had always thought of such wallpaper removal and library research as safe and unrelated enterprises, until a recent experience at the New Hampshire State Library revealed to me their joint hazard.

I discovered there a book with the most intriguing title of *Shadows From the Walls of Death*, which wasn't an Edgar Allan Poe story, but a large pamphlet on the dangers of wallpaper that utilized *arsenic paint!* As I read this monograph, clouds of dust rose from the musty old pages, which must not have been turned in seventy-five years. The text of the work consisted of case histories of the dire consequences certain unfortunate individuals had suffered by inhaling the dust emanating from arsenical wallpaper. This was admittedly dull reading but was largely compensated for by the striking color plates of wallpaper decorated with eerily intense shades of green and blue. It wasn't until I had nearly finished the work that the terrible truth dawned on me. The striking plates were *real* pieces of wallpaper and the dust that lay thick about me was the very lethal emanation to which the author had alluded. Although nothing appears to be wrong with me at present, I live in constant dread of my teeth falling out or my hair turning green. If in the course of stripping the walls of your pre-1880 old-house of their paper, you come upon a layer with intriguing green or blue figures, don't pause too long to contemplate it, but remember that it's The Wall of Death itself!

12

Restoration, Renovation, or Euthanasia?

Now that you've learned the most intimate secrets of the body and soul of your old-house, you're in the privileged position of deciding its fate. It's all too tempting to make such an important decision on the basis of strong emotion and scanty evidence in one's first enchantment (or disillusionment) with an old-house, but this tendency should be strongly resisted. The philosophic approach you take toward your old-house should indeed be colored by your feeling for it, but it also must be based on a sound appraisal of its age, condition, value, and historic or architectural interest.

A recent cartoon shows a man and woman staring bewilderedly at a lot littered with the rotten remnants of what may once have been an old-house, capped by a sign proclaiming: "Another beautiful historic house waiting to be restored!" This "house" was obviously a prime candidate for euthanasia, or mercy killing, yet its owner was trying to find someone gullible enough to buy and resuscitate it. But this was only a cartoon—no one would *really* be so foolish, or would they?

Shortly after asking this question, I found the answer in a newspaper that extravagantly praised a couple who had "restored" an old-house, even though all that remained of it was a piece of the foundation, a fragment of its fireplace, and a photograph! The resuscitation of such scanty remains is technically known as reconstruction and is rarely advisable on either historical, architectural, or economic grounds.

152

Few old houses pose problems as great as this, when they do they are candidates for euthanasia!

It surely wouldn't have been necessary to warn anyone of the shortcomings of this overly solicitous attitude toward old-houses two or three decades ago Old-houses were at that time routinely torn down merely because they were *old houses*, regardless of their condition or intrinsic merit. The decision to put an old-house "out of its misery" should never be made without a most careful assessment of its nature and condition, lest (in the words of American architect George Stephen) "what may be charitably intended as a sort of 'mercy killing' becomes another architectural murder."

I certainly hope and trust that your old-house isn't in such pitiable condition that it could warrant either its reconstruction or destruction. It's far more likely that it will require far less drastic measures than these, such as one of the following alternatives, which will undoubtedly be more appropriate for your particular needs.

Restoration. Although it's often used in a far looser sense, restoration is really the attempt to make a building appear *exactly* as it did at a particular point or period in history. It's usually an expensive alternative and often necessitates the ruthless destruction of notable architectural features from periods other than the one selected. If this predates plumbing, electric wiring, or central heating, these conveniences can't be included in the house. Restoration is thus rarely a viable option for the old-house owner, but is more suitable for buildings of great historic interest open to the public, such as museums.

Renovation and **remodeling.** These are commonly used terms for a philosophy of old-house work that has a sizeable disregard for historical authenticity. If your old-house has lost—or never had—any features of particular historical or architectural interest and you merely are desirous of making a comfortable up-to-date home out of it, this philosophy may be the right one for you.

153

Here is an old-house as you acquire it. What would you do to it?

Preservation. If on the contrary your old-house has great historical or architectural character which you wish to retain and enhance, an approach which may appeal to you is preservation. In its strictest sense this entails the retention, repair, and maintenance of a building in the state in which it has survived, regardless of the nature of additions or alterations that have been made to it over the years. A philosophy many architects and historians are now recommending for state and national landmarks, preservation requires as much historical authenticity as restoration, but doesn't limit its perspective to but one period of a building's past life.

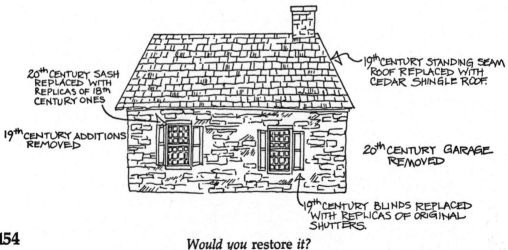

20th CENTURY SASH REPLACED WITH REPLICAS OF 18th CENTURY ONES

19th CENTURY STANDING SEAM ROOF REPLACED WITH CEDAR SHINGLE ROOF.

19th CENTURY ADDITIONS REMOVED

20th CENTURY GARAGE REMOVED

19th CENTURY BLINDS REPLACED WITH REPLICAS OF ORIGINAL SHUTTERS.

Would you restore it?

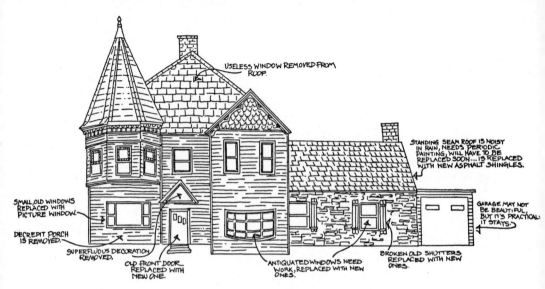

Would you renovate it?

Dynamic Preservation.   Although the most conservative form of preservation doesn't permit the removal of any part of a building (no matter how atrocious it might be) nor does it allow for its future expansion, a far more liberal offshoot of this philosophy does. The proponents of dynamic preservation encourage the retention of the *best* features an old-house has acquired with age, but permit the intelligent removal of discordant architectural notes and condone the construction of harmonious additions. Such a philosophy appears to be an eminently reasonable one for most owners of old-houses.

If your old structure was never a house at all, but was a mill, school, or church, it obviously can't be restored, renovated, or preserved if you intend to live in it. As such intentions have become increasingly common in recent years, due to the

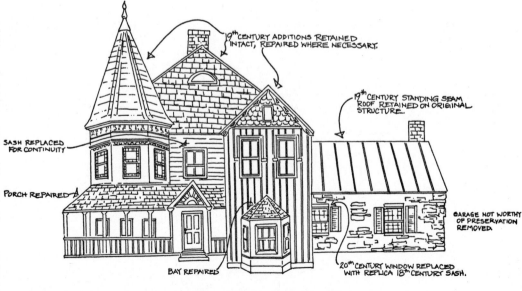

Or would you preserve it?

abundance of these buildings on the market (caused by technical obsolescence, centralization, and spiritual apathy), preservationists have encouraged their adaptive use for purposes other than those for which they were originally intended. As much of the architectural integrity of the building should be preserved as is consistent with its new life (you should make a particular effort to preserve its exterior appearance where possible), while necessary alterations and improvements may be made with clear conscience.

Although it's difficult to advise you what would constitute a "necessary" alteration to your old-house, I would like to emphasize the importance of one guideline, equally applicable to all old-house philosophies. (With the notable exception of that misguided practice—fortunately largely of the past—of "improving" an old-house beyond recognition, known as redesign. See illustration.) As far more damage has been done to old-houses by well-meaning errors of commission than by those of omission, always resist the impulse to change them any more than you absolutely have to. If you have any doubt at all about adding or subtracting an architectural feature from your old-house, *don't do it*—it's safer, quicker, easier and more economical that way.

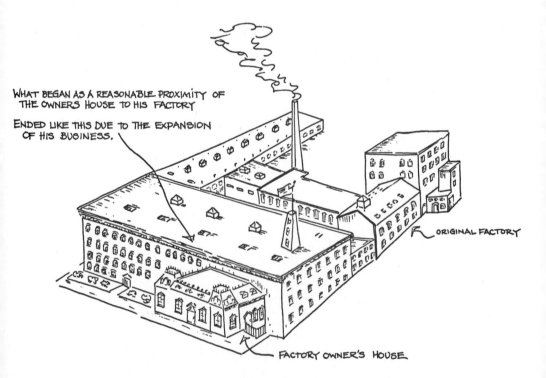

WHAT BEGAN AS A REASONABLE PROXIMITY OF THE OWNERS HOUSE TO HIS FACTORY

ENDED LIKE THIS DUE TO THE EXPANSION OF HIS BUSINESS.

ORIGINAL FACTORY

FACTORY OWNER'S HOUSE.

What would you do to this *old-house? Would it be a case for* adaptive use, *restoration or* . . . ?

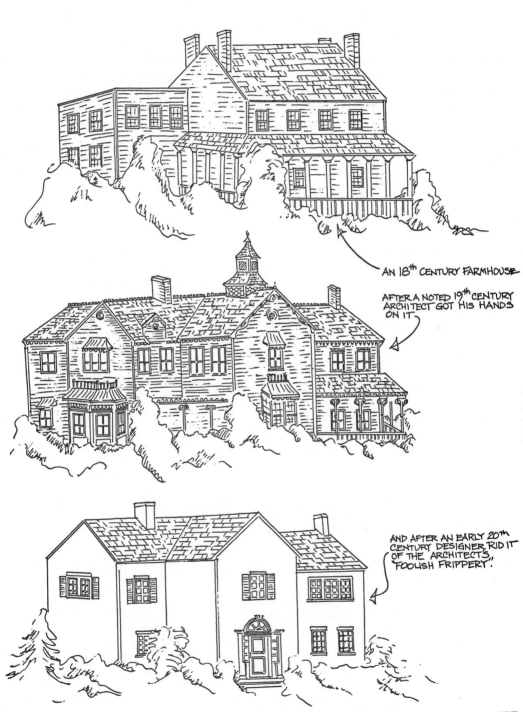

AN 18ᵗʰ CENTURY FARMHOUSE

AFTER A NOTED 19ᵗʰ CENTURY ARCHITECT GOT HIS HANDS ON IT

AND AFTER AN EARLY 20ᵗʰ CENTURY DESIGNER RID IT OF THE ARCHITECT'S "FOOLISH FRIPPERY".

Redesign, *an unfortunate old-house philosophy of the past*

Despite my earlier admonition against a purely emotional basis for old-house philosophy, I don't wish to even slightly discourage the feeling you probably have for your house—for this is the true heart of any philosophy. If you merely think of it as an aggregate of architectural, technical, historical, and financial details, you will never be able to enter into the warm friendship with your house so vital to your relationship. Old-houses can at times be frustrating and disappointing; but if they are your friends, each frustration will resolve itself into an expansion of your capacities for patience, love and understanding—the very qualities that will ensure the continuance and deepening of your friendship!

Old House Transplants: Locating Materials for Your Old-House

One of the greatest rewards you can get for the loving care you may have lavished on your old-house is paradoxically to have it appear that you've done nothing to it at all! In order to achieve such a result, your repairs or improvements must blend so harmoniously with it as to make it impossible to tell the old from the new. This is only possible if you refrain from using unsuitable modern materials in your work. (The worst of these are perhaps plywood paneling, hollow-core flush doors, and aluminum siding.) Such substitutions will clash terribly with your old-house: It will reject them in much the same manner as our bodies refuse to accept organ transplants of the wrong tissue type.

Yet suitable materials for your old-house aren't always available at your local lumberyard, so how do you procure them? I recently had the good fortune to find a donor of such materials next door to a building I was in the process of rehabilitating. It had actually been designed and built in the same year by the same architect and builder as my house, but had partially burned several years previously and had subsequently been abandoned. A more perfect source of vintage materials for the rehabilitation of my old-house couldn't have been found.

I ransacked the half-dead structure for two days, braving the dangers of ravenous rats and collapsing ceilings, but eventually salvaged all the materials my old-house so sorely needed. These included *identical* replacements for several missing or damaged doors, window sash and cornice brackets, and hundreds of feet of flooring, matchboarding, and moldings of exactly the same dimension and **159** configuration as mine. I must confess that I was unusually lucky to have found such a generous donor next door to my house, yet you too might be so fortunate if you keep your eyes and ears open.

If such luck doesn't come your way, the next best alternative would be to find a building of similar vintage to your own which is in the process of being torn down by a demolition contractor. You may then be able to purchase materials right off the site at considerably lower prices than you would have to pay once the contractor had trucked them elsewhere. I once made an arrangement with such a contractor whereby he agreed to pull all the nails out of the lumber I had selected and deliver it to my house at no extra charge. I obtained from him in this manner a number of fine old paneled doors, flooring, a staircase, and dozens of thirty-two-foot timbers. (Try asking for these at your local lumberyard!)

If neither of these possibilities materializes, you may still go to the storage yard of a demolition contractor and purchase from him there at a higher price. If the materials have been there quite a while, make certain they aren't decayed where they came in contact with the ground. Likewise, make sure that doors and sash aren't warped by being stored carelessly, for if they are you'll never straighten them again.

You might also pay a visit to a country sawmill, where you may often order

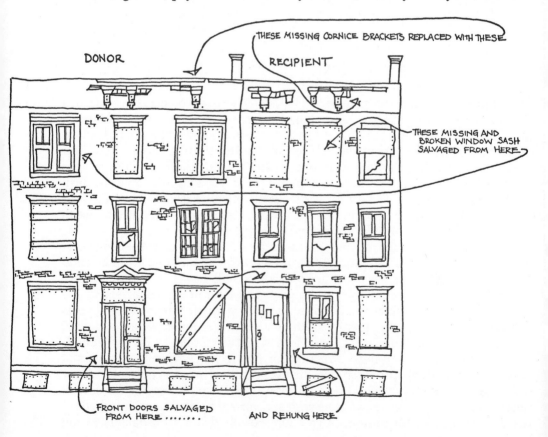

Old-house transplantation

lumber cut and sometimes planed to your specifications. You can often obtain inexpensive materials that are highly compatible with your old-house in this way; but you must be prepared to be extremely patient (both for the sawyers to get around to your "nuisance" order and for it to season once they finally do). I've sometimes waited as long as two years for this to transpire, but in the end it was worth the wait. (This was an exceptional case—my last order was delivered within a month.)

Most large wood shops will be able to plane special moldings or make up custom sash or doors for you, but you will usually have to pay them well for the service. Their charges may nevertheless be much more reasonable if there is a large local demand for such orders, as their jigs and cutters would have already been paid for on other jobs.

If none of these options is available to you or suits your needs, there are a vast number of small and large concerns (most of which have come into being during the past decade) specifically oriented to filling the needs of the old-house owner. This is the most expensive end of the market, but it also can be the most convenient and in some cases the *only* alternative. Most of these businesses sell reproductions, but some handle "architectural antiques" at prices many times

A healthy house again, thanks to its donor

what you would pay to a demolition contractor. It's nevertheless possible to obtain items from such dealers that you may not be able to locate anywhere else, so they do provide a valuable service.

These concerns offer a large variety of old-house specialties, including:

Hand-forged iron hardware
Victorian millwork
Embossed tin ceilings
Hand-hewn beams
Decorative plasterwork
Victorian handprinted wallpaper
Antique radiators

Wide pine boards
Old bricks
Custom-made shutters and blinds
Handcrafted solid wood toilet seats
Fancy cut shingles
Embossed brass hardware
Antique lighting fixtures

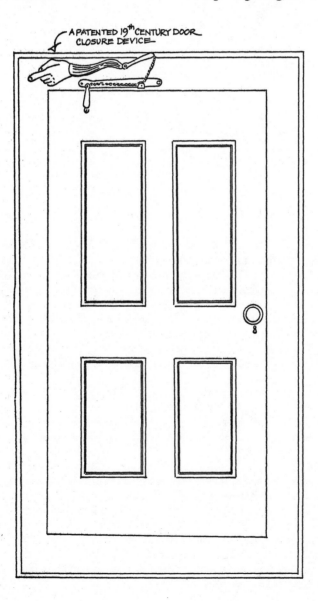

A PATENTED 19th CENTURY DOOR CLOSURE DEVICE

Bibliography

Advisory Service of Greater Portland Landmarks, *Living With Old Houses* (Portland, Maine: Greater Portland Landmarks, 1975).

Association for Preservation Technology, *Bulletin of the Association for Preservation Technology* (Ottowa, Ontario, Canada: Association for Preservation Technology, Quarterly). Technical journal for restorationists and preservationists.

Baer, Morley, Pomada, Elizabeth, and Larsen, Michael, *Painted Ladies: San Francisco's Resplendent Victorians* (New York: Dutton, 1978).

Baker, Roy W., "To Keep an Old House in Good Standing," *Old-time New England* (Spring 1956). Structural repair to a braced-frame house by a well-qualified old-time restorationist.

Blandy, Thomas, and Lamoureaux, Denis, *All Through the House, A Guide to Home Weatherization* (New York: McGraw-Hill, 1980).

Browne, Dan, *The Renovation Book* (New York: McGraw-Hill, 1976).

Bracken, John, and Stone, Linda, *Restoring the Victorian House* (San Francisco: Chronicle Books, 1981).

Bullock, Orin M., *The Restoration Manual* (Norwalk, Connecticut: Silvermine, 1966). An architect's excellent account of his responsibilities during the restoration of a house.

Candee, Richard M., "Preparing and Mixing Colors In 1812," *Antiques*, (April 1978).

_____, "The Rediscovery of Milk-based House Paints and the Myth of 'Brickdust and Buttermilk' Paints," *Old-time New England* 57 (Winter 1968).

Carpenters' Company of the City and County of Philadelphia, eds., *Building Early America* (Radnor, Pennsylvania: Chilton Book Co., 1976). Good articles on the development of central heating, the manufacture of window glass, early roofing materials, masonry techniques, and house framing.

Carter, Joe, ed., *Solarizing Your Present Home* (Emmaus, Pennsylvania: Rodale Press, 1981).

Condit, Carl W., *American Building: Materials and Techniques from the First Colonial Settlements to the Present* (Chicago: University of Chicago Press, 1968).

Cummings, Abbot Lowell, *The Framed Houses of Massachusetts Bay 1625–1725* (Cambridge, Massachusetts: The Belknap Press of Harvard University Press, 1979).

Day, Richard, *The Practical Handbook of Plumbing and Heating* (Rockville, Maryland: Fawcett, 1969).

Fahy, Christopher, *Home Remedies* (New York: Scribner's, 1975). The author's experience in rehabilitating several old houses.

Ferro, Maximilian F., *How to Care for Your Old Building in New Bedford* (New Bedford, Massachusetts: City of New Bedford, 1977).

Fitch, James Marston, *American Building: The Environmental Forces That Shaped It* (Boston: Houghton Mifflin, 1972). Fitch draws interesting parallels between the house and the human body.

Fjelstul, Alice Bancroft, and Schad, Patricia Brown, *Early American Wall Stencils in Color* (New York: Dutton, 1982).

Foley, Mary Mix, *The American House* (New York: Harper and Row, Colophon Books, 1980). A manual of architectural styles.

Gay, Larry, ed., *The Complete Book of Insulating* (Brattleboro, Vermont: The Stephen Crane Press, 1980).

Graham, Frank D., ed., *Audels Carpenters and Builders Guide* (New York: Theo. Audel & Co., 1945).

———, *Audels House Heating Guide* (New York: Theo. Audel & Co., 1948).

———, *Audels Masons and Builders Guide* (New York: Theo. Audel & Co., 1936).

———, *Audels Plumbers and Steamfitters Guide* (New York: Theo. Audel & Co., 1945). The earlier editions of these Audel guides are a most valuable source of information on old tools, materials, and techniques relevant to old-houses. Most of the later editions are disappointing.

Hart, G. Kimball, and the editors of U.S. News and World Report Books, *How to Cut Your Energy Costs* (Washington, D.C.: U.S. News and World Report Books, 1978).

Highland, Harold Joseph, *Audels Painting and Decorating Manual* (New York: Theo. Audel & Co., 1965). Although not one of the previously mentioned "earlier editions," this is pretty sound information on house painting.

Historic Salem, Inc., *The Salem Handbook: A Renovation Guide for Homeowners* (Salem, Massachusetts: Historic Salem Inc., n.d.).

Hoffman, George, *How to Inspect a House* (New York: Dell, 1979).

Hotton, Peter, *So You Want to Fix Up an Old House* (Boston: Little, Brown, 1979).

Hudobar, Michael, *The Artifact Hunter's Handbook* (Chicago: Contemporary Books Inc., 1979). Written from the point of view of the collector of artifacts, rather than from that of the professional archaeologist.

Hume, Ivor Noel, *Artifacts of Colonial America* (New York: Knopf, 1970). A professional archaeologist tells how to identify artifacts and use them for dating purposes.

Hutchins, Nigel, *Restoring Old Houses* (New York: Van Nostrand Reinhold, 1980).

Johnston, H. R., Smith, Virgil K., and Beal, Raymond H., *Subterranean Termites, Their Prevention and Control in Buildings*, U.S. Dept. of Agriculture Home & Garden Bulletin #64. (Washington, D.C.: Government Printing Office, 1977).

Kangas, Robert, *The Old-house Rescue Book* (Reston, Virginia: Reston Publishing Co., 1982).

Kelly, J. Frederick, *Early Domestic Architecture of Connecticut* (New York: Dover, 1963). A classic work (originally published by Yale University Press in 1924) with excellent detailed drawings.

King, A. Rowden, *Realtor's Guide to Architecture, How to Identify and Sell Every Kind of Home* (Englewood Cliffs, New Jersey: Prentice-Hall, 1954).

Labine, Clem, and staff of *Old-House Journal*, eds., *The Old-House Compendium* (Woodstock, New York: Overlook Press, 1980). A selection of articles which previously appeared in *The Old-House Journal*.

Lancaster, Clay, "Some Secret Spaces and Private Places in Early American Architecture," *Antiques* 50 (November 1946). One of the few articles on secret rooms and staircases.

Litchfield, Michael W., *Renovation: A Complete Guide* (New York: Wiley, 1982). A remarkably complete coverage of building skills, although the author doesn't appear to have a deep commitment to or understanding of old-houses, despite the color photographs of intriguing old-house details. Heartily recommended nonetheless.

Little, Nina Fletcher, *American Decorative Wall Painting 1700–1850* (New York: Dutton, 1972).

———, "Finding the Records of an Old House," *Old-Time New England* 40 (October 1949).

Long, Charles K., *The Stonebuilder's Primer* (Camden East, Ontario, Canada: Camden House, 1981).

McAlester, Virginia, and McAlester, Lee, *A Field Guide to American Houses* (New York: Knopf, 1984). An excellent compendium of architectural styles of American residences from 17th century to date.

McKee, Harley J., *Introduction to Early American Masonry* (New York: National Trust for Historic Preservation and Columbia University, 1973). Well-researched information on early American stone and brickwork, mortar, and plaster.

McPartland, Joseph F., *McGraw-Hill's National Electrical Code Handbook* (18th ed.) (New York: McGraw-Hill, 1984). McPartland's extensive rewriting of the NEC *almost* makes it appear lucid.

Marshall, Brian, and Argue, Robert, *The Super Insulated Retrofit Book* (Toronto: Renewable Energy in Canada, 1981).

Massey, Howard C., *Basic Plumbing with Illustrations* (Carlsbad, California: Craftsman Book Co., 1980).

Mercer, Henry, *Ancient Carpenters' Tools* (Doylestown, Pennsylvania: Bucks County Historical Society, 1960). The classic well-researched work on early American woodworking tools and their antecedents.

———, "The Dating of Old Houses," *Old-Time New England* 15 (April 1924). A well-researched article on dating American houses until around 1850. Not pertinent to dating late-19th or 20th-century structures.

Mix, Floyd M., *House Wiring Simplified* (South Holland, Illinois: Goodheart-Willcox, 1981).

Moore, Harry B., *Wood-inhabiting Insects in Houses: Their Identification, Biology, Prevention and Control* (Washington, D.C.: Government Printing Office, 1979). A joint publication of USDA, US Forest Service, and HUD, the best work on the subject that I've seen.

Mullin, Ray C., *Electrical Wiring Residential* (New York: Van Nostrand Reinhold, 1981).

Nash, George, *Old-houses, A Rebuilder's Manual* (Englewood Cliffs, New Jersey: Prentice Hall, 1980). Contains one of the few detailed accounts of the use of house jacks.

National Trust for Historic Preservation, *Historic Preservation* (Washington, D.C.: National Trust for Historic Preservation). Bimonthly nontechnical preservation magazine.

National Bureau of Standards and U.S. Department of Commerce, in cooperation with the Federal Energy Administration, *Retrofitting Existing Homes for Energy Conservation: An Economic Analysis* (Washington, D.C.: Government Printing Office, 1974).

Nielsen, Sally E., *Insulating the Old House* (Portland, Maine: Greater Portland Landmarks, 1979).

Old-House Journal Corp., *The Old-House Journal* (Brooklyn, New York: Old-House Journal Corp.). A monthly newsletter of great interest to the owner of an old-house. The best and only of its kind.

Old-House Journal Newsletter, *The Old-House Journal Catalog* (Brooklyn, New York: Old-House Journal Corp.). An annual directory of old-house materials and services.

Oman, Charles C., and Hamilton, Jean, *Wallpapers: An International Survey from the Victoria and Albert Museum* (New York: Abrams, 1982). As many early American wallpapers were imported from England, this lavishly illustrated book is very appropriate.

Ordish, George, *The Living American House* (New York: William Morrow, 1981). Unusual account of the insect population of an old house.

Organic Gardening and Farming, *Build it Better Yourself* (Emmaus, Pennsylvania, Rodale Press, 1977). Although primarily devoted to farm projects, contains one of the few accounts of replacing heavy timber sills and posts.

Ortho Books, *Basic Plumbing Techniques* (San Francisco: Ortho Books, 1982).

———, *Basic Wiring Techniques* (San Francisco: Ortho Books, 1982).

Palmquist, Roland E., *Audels Guide to the 1984 National Electrical Code* (Indianapolis: Bobbs-Merrill, 1984).

Peirce, Josephine H., *Fire on the Hearth* (Springfield, Massachusetts: Pond-Ekberg Co., 1951). Includes a well-researched account of the development of the American woodstove.

Phillips, Morgan, and Whitney, Christopher, "The Restoration of Original Paints at Otis House," *Old-Time New England* 62 (Summer 1971).

Plunkett, Mrs. H. M., *Women, Plumbers and Doctors* (New York: D. Appleton & Co., 1900). One of the many tracts of the time promoting greater household concern with sanitation.

Price, Billy L., and Price, James T., *Homeowner's Guide to Saving Energy* (revised ed.) (Blue Ridge Summit, Pennsylvania: TAB Books, 1981).

Reece, Beverly A., "Getting to Know an Old House," *Historic Preservation* 31 (Sept.–Oct. 1979): 43–47.

Rooney, William F., *Practical Guide to Home Restoration* (New York: Bantam/Hudson Idea Books, 1980).

Rusk, Katherine, *Renovating the Victorian House: A Guide for Aficionados of Old Houses* (San Francisco: One Hundred One Productions, 1981).

Sanborn, Kate, *Old Time Wall Papers* (Greenwich, Connecticut: Literary Collector Press, 1905).

Smith, Baird M., "Conserving Energy in Historic Buildings," *Construction Specifier* (November 1978).

Society for the Preservation of New England Antiquities, *Old-Time New England* (Boston: Society for the Preservation of New England Antiquities. A semiannual journal of restoration and preservation in New England.

Socolow, Robert H., ed., *Saving Energy in the Home: Princeton's Experiments at Twin Rivers* (Cambridge, Massachusetts: Ballinger Publishing Co., 1978).

Spielvogel, Lawrence G., "Exploding Some Myths About Building Energy Use," *Architectural Record* (February 1976).

Sprague, Paul E., "The Origin of Balloon Framing," *Journal of the Society of Architectural Historians* 40 (December 1981).

Stephen, George, *Remodeling Old Houses Without Destroying Their Character* (New York: Knopf, 1973). Written by an architect who is sensitive to the spirit of old-houses.

Strickler, Darryl J., *Passive Solar Retrofit* (New York: Van Nostrand Reinhold, 1982).

Sullivan, George, *Discover Archaeology* (Garden City, New York: Doubleday, 1980). A good introduction to the subject.

Summers, Lydia B., et al. *Researching the Old House* (Portland, Maine: Greater Portland Landmarks, 1981).

Technical Preservation Services Division, Heritage Conservation & Recreation Service, *Preservation Briefs* (Washington, D.C.: Government Printing Office). Published periodically.

Time-Life Books, *The Old House* (Alexandria, Virginia: Time-Life, 1980).

Time-Life Books, *Basic Wiring* (Alexandria, Virginia: Time-Life, 1980).

U.S. Dept. of Agriculture, *The Old House Borer*, U.S. Dept. of Agriculture Leaflet #501 (Washington, D.C.: Government Printing Office, n.d.).

———, Forest Products Laboratory, *Wood Handbook* (Washington, D.C.: Government Printing Office, 1974). Chapter 17 contains good information on "protection from organisms that degrade wood."

U.S. Dept. of Housing & Urban Development, *In the Bank . . . Or Up the Chimney?* (Washington, D.C.: Government Printing Office, 1975). Unusually helpful home energy conservation pamphlet.

Van Den Branden, F., and Hartsell, Thomas L., *Plastering, Skill and Practice* (Chicago: American Technical Society, 1971).

Verrall, Arthur, and Amburgey, Terry, *Prevention and Control of Decay in Homes* (Washington, D.C.: Government Printing Office, 1980). Another very useful government publication, a joint publication of the USDA, US Forest Service and HUD.

Villa, Bob, and Davison, Jane, *This Old House* (Boston: Little Brown, 1980). Well-written account of the rehabilitation of an old house; taken from the television series.

Walker, Lester, *American Shelter* (Woodstock, New York: Overlook Press, 1981). The most engaging book on architectural classification I've seen; excellent drawings.

Warner Books, *The Brand New Old House Catalogue* (New York: Warner Books, 1980).

Webber, Joan W., *How Old Is Your House? A Guide to Research* (Chester, Connecticut: Pequot Press, 1978).

_____, *How to Live with Your Old House* (New York: McGraw-Hill, 1981).

Williams, Henry Lionel, and Williams, Ottalie K., *A Guide to Old American Houses 1700–1900* (New York: A. S. Barnes, 1962).

_____, *Old American Houses: How to Restore, Remodel and Reproduce Them* (New York: Coward-McCann, 1957). This was for many years practically the only book on the subject addressing itself to the house-owner.

Wilson, Scott, *The Plumber's Bible* (Garden City, New York: Doubleday, 1981).

Wilson, Tom, ed., *Home Remedies, A Guide-book for Residential Retrofit* (Philadelphia: Mid-Atlantic Solar Energy Association, 1981).

Wing, Charles, *From the Walls In* (Boston: Little Brown, 1979). Principles of retrofitting, written by an expert in the field.

Wright, Lawrence, *Clean and Decent* (New York: Viking, 1960). An engaging account of the history of bathrooms, baths, and toilets in the United States, France, and England.

Zamm, Alfred V., M.D. *Why Your House May Endanger Your Health* (New York: Simon & Schuster, 1980). An allergist warns us to beware of certain materials, furnishings, and methods of construction in our houses.

Index

(Page numbers shown in italic [e.g., *37*] indicate an illustration.)